The Retail Prices Index

Jeff Ralph • Robert O'Neill
Paul A. Smith

The Retail Prices Index

A Short History

palgrave
macmillan

Jeff Ralph
University of Southampton
Southampton, UK

Robert O'Neill
University of Manchester
Manchester, UK

Paul A. Smith
University of Southampton
Southampton, UK

ISBN 978-3-030-46562-9 ISBN 978-3-030-46563-6 (eBook)
https://doi.org/10.1007/978-3-030-46563-6

This Palgrave Pivot imprint is published by the registered company Springer Nature Switzerland AG.
The registered company address is: Gewerbestrasse 11, 6330 Cham, Switzerland

Preface

The story of the Retail Prices Index (RPI) is a dramatic one. The RPI was first produced in interim form in June 1947, and in its full form from January 1956. Over the next 40 years it was gradually improved through the development of its methodology together with an expansion of the basket of goods and services. Its use also grew to encompass the adjustment of wages, pensions, benefits and government bonds in response to overall changes in prices. It remained the sole measure of inflation in consumer prices until 1996 when the need for a common measure of inflation across the member states of the European Union led to the introduction of a new measure—the Harmonised Index of Consumer Prices. In the UK this new measure was first published in 1997 and became known as the Consumer Prices Index (CPI) and aspects of its methodology differed from the RPI, resulting in a different estimate for inflation when the two indices were calculated using the same data, the CPI usually being smaller. The main cause of the difference, the use of different formulas, became known as the "formula effect" and became one of the most debated technical topics in official statistics.

In 2010, two changes started a chain of events that would result in the RPI losing its National Statistics status. Firstly, a perceived problem in clothing inflation led to a change in collection instructions intended to improve the capture of clothing prices; this unexpectedly led to a widening of the gap between RPI inflation and CPI inflation from 0.54 percentage points to 0.86—a considerable change. Secondly, the government decided to switch the indexation of state pensions and some benefits from the RPI to the CPI, using the justification that the CPI was a more appropriate measure to use. With CPI inflation being lower than RPI inflation, many people would lose in the future as benefits and pensions would increase at a slower rate due to indexation with the CPI rather than the RPI. The combination of these two events raised the profile of the two indices and their different estimates of consumer price inflation to wide public notice.

In August 2010, the Royal Statistical Society wrote to the UK Statistics Authority expressing concern about the differences between the measures; they urged an investigation into the issue and, in particular, the use of different formulas. In response, the Office for National Statistics (ONS) began a two year programme of research, with independent advice provided by external experts to supplement the work of the ONS. By 2012, the ONS concluded that it was the methodology of the RPI that was at fault, particularly a specific formula (the average of price relatives) that was causing an upwards bias. The UK Statistics Authority presented options for changing the way the RPI was produced and launched a public consultation. It included the option to leave the RPI unchanged.

Changing an indexation measure is not a simple matter. The long history of use of the RPI meant that it was embedded in a wide variety of financial arrangements. These included forming the basis for wage negotiations, the adjustment of benefits, pensions, contracts and some government bonds. In some cases, such as private pensions and index-linked government bonds, these were long-term commitments where the expectation of beneficiaries was for long-term stability in the means of indexation.

The public consultation resulted in a large number of respondents stating that they wished the RPI to remain unchanged. Some respondents with economic and statistical expertise disagreed with the technical assessment of the ONS that the RPI was at fault. In responding to the views captured by the consultation, the National Statistician (Jill Matheson) acknowledged demand for stability in the measure while accepting the ONS view that the RPI was a poor measure of inflation; she announced that the RPI would continue unchanged to meet legacy uses. In addition, she strongly encouraged a move away from the use of the RPI to the CPI.

What was the government's response to this advice? The government had already started to change its preferred indexation measure from the RPI to the CPI in 2010 and after 2012 it continued, proceeding in a cautious manner so as to protect revenue for the Exchequer. A few new uses of the RPI by government were introduced, but in response to criticism, the Chancellor of the Exchequer promised that this would stop. For private pensions, the use of the RPI has remained in place despite legal challenges by some companies trying to switch the indexing measure from the RPI to the CPI to limit pension liabilities and make the schemes more sustainable. For government bonds, a material change away from the RPI, or a material change to the methodology of the RPI, would trigger the option for bond-holders to ask for redemption of bonds at potentially considerable expense to the Exchequer. This was a powerful disincentive to make changes.

The government looked at the potential to change the indexing of private pensions, overriding pension agreements. It has also considered issuing CPI indexed bonds to sit alongside existing RPI indexed bonds. However, in both cases there were difficulties and it decided against change. This had the effect of maintaining the use of an officially discredited index with seemingly no end in sight. This situation attracted criticism from many stakeholders, including the Governor of the Bank of England. In response, the House of Lords Economic Affairs Committee carried out an inquiry, delivering a highly critical report at the start of 2019. This prompted the UK Statistics Authority to write to the Chancellor of the Exchequer proposing modifications to the RPI. The Chancellor has accepted that the RPI in its current form must change, but has delayed consent until 2030 at the latest and 2025 at the earliest.

This book tells the story of the RPI, from the early developments that preceded its inception, to its foundations after the Second World War, its subsequent development and the sequence of events that led to it losing its National Statistics status. Chapter 1 introduces the concept of the level of prices, how it is measured and the uses of such a measure. Chapter 2 gives a brief description of the early developments that established the foundations of inflation measurement in the Nineteenth Century, through the creation of the first official measure at the start of the First World War; the chapter ends with a description of the creation of an interim index of retail prices just after the Second World War. Chapter 3 describes the introduction of the Retail Prices Index and the development of the index in its early years. The further development of the RPI is covered in Chap. 4; this includes the addition of measures of owner occupiers' housing costs to the index, improvements to local price collection and the publication of sub-indices. Chapter 5 describes the impact of the introduction of the CPI, the response to the influential Boskin Report from the US and the differences between the RPI and CPI. It also considers inflation measures and their uses from a political viewpoint. The dramatic events from 2009 to 2013 are the subject of Chap. 6—this covers the events that led to the RPI losing its National Statistics status in 2013. Lastly, Chap. 7 considers the events of the years 2014 onwards with the Johnson Review, government consultations on private pension indexing and index-linked bonds. It ends with the 2018–2019 House of Lords inquiry and the official response.

In order to deliver a short description of the history, the extent of the exploration of the historical background is necessarily limited. A much fuller account can be found in our previous book (O'Neill et al. 2017). The description of how a measure of inflation is produced is kept very brief and we have not included any of the mathematical details behind the calculations of the two measures; Appendix A gives the basic details of the formulas. An introductory guide to how inflation measures are produced is available from the ONS (2017); our previous book on Index Numbers (Ralph et al. 2015) also provides both background information and mathematical details. We also provide a timeline of events in Appendix B.

In writing this book, we have consulted a range of sources. Firstly, all three authors have worked for the Office for National Statistics and have personal experience to draw on. Secondly, many helpful papers are available on-line from the ONS and the National Archives including the RPI Advisory Committee papers. To gain a more detailed view of past events, we have consulted many paper files in the National Archives. Thirdly, we have benefited from the personal experience of colleagues who worked on price statistics going back to the 1970s. In combining such a large volume of information into a relatively short book we have had to summarise many complex and interesting topics. Extensive references are provided for those readers who would like to follow up on specific topics.

Southampton, UK — Jeff Ralph
Manchester, UK — Robert O'Neill
Southampton, UK — Paul A. Smith

References

O'Neill, R., Ralph, J., & Smith P. A. (2017). *Inflation: History and measurement.* Basingstoke: Palgrave Macmillan.

ONS. (2017). *Consumer price indices, a brief guide: 2017.* Retrieved February 19, 2020, from https://www.ons.gov.uk/economy/inflationandpriceindices/articles/consumerpriceindicesabriefguide/2017.

Ralph, J., O'Neill, R., & Winton, J. (2015). *A practical introduction to index numbers.* Chichester: Wiley.

Acknowledgements

We would like to thank our former colleagues at the Office for National Statistics, both those currently working there and those who have retired, for answering our many questions about the developments in consumer price statistics. In particular, we'd like to thank the staff in Prices Division for their generous help. Any errors in the text are, of course, the responsibility of the authors.

We have consulted very many documents in writing this book and we are grateful for the support of the library staff from our respective Universities and also to the staff at the National Archives. Thanks are due also to our partners Bryony, Sarah and Mila for their support and encouragement together with an extraordinary level of patience.

We would also like to thank Palgrave Macmillan for their expert handling of the manuscript.

Finally, we'd like to note that the views expressed in this book are those of the authors and not necessarily those of the organisations for which they work.

Contents

List of Figures

List of Tables

CHAPTER 1

Introduction

Abstract Here we introduce the measurement of changes in prices, and the key events which prompted the development of consumer price measurement in the United Kingdom and led to the Retail Prices Index (RPI). We discuss some of the important uses of the RPI, which have made it an essential component of economic management, and the effects of changes in the way prices are measured. More recently, the introduction and use of the Consumer Prices Index (CPI) has made debate around the measurement of inflation more contentious. We consider how this has polarised opinions, and highlight the need for a period of stability.

Keywords Value of money • Inflation targeting • Indexation measures

1.1 Prices, the Value of Money and Indexation

The prices of consumer goods and services affect us all. From our individual experiences of shopping we know that prices change and the popular view is that prices tend to rise over time. For some goods such as petrol and diesel, prices are particularly volatile, with rises and falls driven by the price of oil, which is sensitive to political developments across the world and other market factors. The oil price is an important economic indicator and changes are reported in the press along with their implications for motorists. Consumers who buy petrol or diesel regularly will be aware of

J. Ralph et al., *The Retail Prices Index*,
https://doi.org/10.1007/978-3-030-46563-6_1

the resulting price changes. For other items such as bread and milk, prices are usually more stable over time and changes are not so apparent or newsworthy.

Although the common perception is that, overall, prices go up, we as individual consumers cannot see the whole picture extending over the huge range of consumer goods and services on offer in the marketplace. A robust statistical treatment is the only way of knowing if, overall, prices are rising or falling. The Retail Prices Index (RPI) is one of a family of statistical measures that attempts to address this question. It is constructed by taking a basket of goods and services carefully chosen to represent the full extent of the products and services available for consumers to buy and tracking prices of the component items. Each month, prices of these representative items are captured across the UK in different types of store and from the internet. The proportions of expenditure on different types of consumer item are also measured, though less frequently, primarily through a household survey. The average price change from a given reference period (usually a calendar month) is calculated by adding together the prices changes of the representative items weighted by the proportion of household expenditure they, and the items they represent, take up.

The Retail Prices Index has been calculated on a monthly basis since January 1956 and shows how prices have changed each month from a reference period where the index value is set to 100. The original reference period was January 1956; it is revised from time to time with the current reference period being January 1987. A convenient way to report price change is to calculate the percentage change in the Retail Prices Index for each month from the same month a year ago; this is reported as the (twelve-month) "rate of inflation". If we look at the average value of inflation as calculated from the RPI from January 1993 to October 2019, we find prices have risen on average by 2.8% a year, approximately consistent with a doubling of prices over 25 years. The popular perception that, overall, prices tend to rise is correct. Of course, price rises haven't been constant over these 322 months. Although the average value of inflation is relatively small at 2.8%, it reached 5.6% in September 2011 and inflation was negative between March and October 2009, during the great recession. The all-time highest inflation rate for the UK, as measured by the RPI, was 26.9% which occurred in August 1975.

High values of inflation can be highly damaging and even modest values cause problems. This is clear to see from a simple example. Consider an annual salary of £26,416, which was the average annual regular pay before tax for Great Britain in September 2019 (ONS 2019a). We can say that this has a certain purchasing power, that is, we can buy a range of goods and services with it. With an annual inflation rate of 2.8%, after 5 years, the purchasing power of this salary would be £23,009 (at the level of prices when the salary was first measured). This effect of inflation is widely understood and governments and employers (usually) adjust benefits, pensions, salaries and thresholds to account for the effects of inflation. This process of adjusting financial quantities by a measure of inflation is called "indexation" and it seeks to maintain the value of money in response to overall price change.

From our position today, we mostly take the measurement of inflation and the important process of indexation for granted. However, reaching this position has taken over three hundred years of development.

1.2 The Road to Modern Inflation Measurement

Price changes and their potentially damaging effects were first studied at the start of the eighteenth century and by the 1830s a clear statement of the issues and a proposal for a remedy was made by the Scottish political economist Joseph Lowe. The remedy was the measurement of the general level of prices and its application to make adjustments to financial instruments. While recognising the problem and what would be needed to find a solution was clearly an important step, it would take another eighty years for such a measure to be put in place.

From the 1830s onwards, a number of insightful individuals overlapping the areas of Economics and Statistics developed both the theory and practice required to produce an inflation measure. While individuals and private organisations began the practice of collecting data on a limited scale, it became apparent that the resources of the state would be required to move towards a robust measure. The role of the state in inflation measurement developed from the 1880s, when the Board of Trade began the systematic collection of both retail prices of goods bought by working class households and the proportions of household expenditure taken up by various items. The first measure of the general level of prices was introduced at the start of the First World War as the Cost of Living Index relevant to working class households. As an inflation measure, it was in a basic form, but its introduction was a very important step.

The inter-war period saw little development of official inflation measures; it wasn't until after the Second World War that significant improvement was made with the development of the Interim Index of Retail Prices and the subsequent introduction of the Retail Prices Index in 1956. The methodology and the extent of the data collection at this point produced what we can recognise as a "modern" measure of inflation. The following years saw a range of improvements with an expanded basket of goods and services and advances in methodology being amongst the most noticeable changes.

As well as these improvements in the construction of the RPI, so applications of an inflation measure gradually expanded beyond informing wage settlements to include the adjustment of benefits and pensions. Over the years, the uses of indexation have continued to grow so that very large sums of money are now involved in maintaining the purchasing power of wages, pensions, benefits and more complex financial instruments.

Beyond the increased use of the RPI for indexation, developments in economic theory through the 1970s led governments and central banks to adopt explicit inflation targets based on inflation measures in their role of managing the economy through the setting of interest rates.

1.3 Monetarism and Inflation Targetting

Monetarism is a school of economic thought that gained widespread prominence in the 1970s. It is concerned with the role of money in economies; it maintains that the supply of money in an economy is the main determinant of economic growth and the level of prices and that the main role of the state is to manage the money supply accordingly. Governments and central banks have developed policies to control the money supply and to try to ensure both steady economic growth and low levels of inflation, the most prominent of which has been the management of central inflation rates.

It seems intuitive that a zero level of inflation is best; this would require no indexation, and so no money input from employers and the government. However, economists argue that a small level of inflation is beneficial. A small level of inflation is associated with economic growth and a corresponding increase in economic output per capita, which is a driver of increases in wealth. Businesses can also benefit. With small levels of inflation, businesses can decide to either over- or under-compensate workers with wage rises to re-allocate labour to its most productive areas, thus a small amount of inflation can be thought to support the work of the "invisible hand" at work in the market economy.

In practice, governments or central banks with the freedom to make financial adjustments set targets for inflation. In the UK, the Bank of England adopted an inflation target after the UK exited the European Exchange Rate Mechanism in 1992. The target was set at 2.5% as measured by a variant of the RPI. In 1998, the Bank's Monetary Policy Committee was given the responsibility for setting interest rates in order to meet this target as part of the process of the Bank of England becoming an independent institution. The inflation target became 2% in 2003 when the UK government switched the index used for targeting from the RPI to the CPI; the difference in the value of the target reflecting the difference between the RPI and CPI at the time. The current target of 2% is a value used by other countries as well as the UK (O'Neill et al. 2017, pp. 26–32).

1.4 The Uses of Inflation Measures

The first official measure of the general level of prices was produced at the start of the First World War. It was called the working-class Cost of Living Index. Prices were collected from retail outlets that "conducted working class trade" and the goods and services in the basket were considered suitable for working class households. With substantial price rises at the start of the War, the government was concerned that essential war work might be disrupted by industrial unrest. Wage boards, which considered the pay of workers, were encouraged by the government to use the Cost of Living Index as a basis for their deliberations. This was the first use of an inflation measure as a basis for adjusting wages and established the principle of the approach we still use today.

After the War, the index was used more widely, including for the adjustment of wages for public sector workers; it was estimated that by 1922, three million workers were covered by what were called "sliding scales" which linked pay to price changes as indicated by movements in the index. Under these arrangements, when overall prices fell, so wages were lowered. This led to the numbers of workers covered by these arrangements reducing over periods when prices were falling and increasing when prices were rising.

The high levels of inflation in the 1970s show just how important indexation had become. The average value of RPI inflation in the 1970s was 12.7%, with the average value in 1975 reaching 24.1%; in contrast, the average value in 2019 was 2.6%. Without compensating wage rises, the inflation levels in the 1970s would have destroyed the purchasing power of workers' pay. The damaging power of inflation was felt by people who had retired with private pensions before and during the 1970s. For some of these pensioners there was no adjustment for inflation and their wealth was substantially reduced as a result. The statutory indexing of private pensions was only introduced in the early 1980s. The RPI was also used for the indexation of some government bonds; the Bank of England introduced index-linked government debt in 1981. Chapter 4 looks further into the developments of the RPI in the 1970s and 1980s.

The issuance of index-linked government debt from 1981 was an important new application of the RPI. Subsequent years saw further tranches of index-linked debt sold with the size of the index-linked part being about 25% (by value) at the end of December 2018. In some cases, these indexed linked bonds refer explicitly to the RPI as the means of indexation. This use of indexation represents a long-term commitment by the government to those it has borrowed money from. Long term commitments to indexation based on the RPI can also be found in some private pension agreements and in the adjustment of financial elements of commercial contracts which extend over several years.

Looking across the wide range of current uses of inflation measures shows a considerable growth in indexation since the introduction of the RPI in 1956. Joseph Lowe, the Scottish political economist, was prescient in recognising the importance of a measure of the general level of prices and its application in 1823 (see Chap. 2)—it has been a highly beneficial development for workers, pensioners and recipients of benefits and the usefulness of such a measure is rarely questioned, although its measurement sometimes is. Today, the government's overall economic policy relies in part on the rate of inflation and businesses benefit from knowledge of inflation to inform investment decisions. Taken together, these uses demonstrate just how important inflation measures have become to the life of the economy.

The ONS publishes inflation measures every month and considerable care goes into ensuring high quality estimates are produced on time. As well as the need to produce the numbers in a timely manner, there is also a drive to ensure the methodology is the best it can be, given the constraints involved. This is achieved by reviewing the methodology of the index regularly and updating it when the need arises. Underlying research is also commissioned and often leads to improvements being made. While improving the methodology is, of course, a good thing, it can lead to problems, particularly where there are long term applications of statistical measures. This has certainly been the case with measures of inflation in recent years.

1.5 The Effects of Changes in Inflation Measurement

All official statistics are updated from time to time. In some cases, changes are needed to ensure statistics remain relevant. For example, the basket of goods and services used in the measurement of inflation is updated each year with a few new items added and some existing items removed; this ensures that inflation statistics remain relevant to the changing consumer marketplace. These changes are not controversial and can be made without adverse impact on the users of inflation measures.

Having more than one measure may not present difficulties either; for example, where different measures have different purposes. This was the case when versions of the RPI applicable for low income pensioner households were introduced in the 1960s. Having multiple measures can, however, be problematic if they are intended to measure the same quantity, or if they are perceived in this way by those who wish to use them. The RPI was the sole measure of consumer price inflation in the UK for 40 years, until the introduction of the Harmonised Index of Consumer Prices (HICP) in 1996; this was a critical point for UK inflation measurement. Although the HICP was originally produced for the specific purpose of enabling comparison of inflation across member countries of the European Union for the assessment of economic convergence, the UK government saw it as an alternative measure for domestic purposes. Chapter 5 describes the important changes that challenged the dominant position of the RPI as the CPI became a competitor measure.

The UK version of the HICP was named the Consumer Prices Index and it produced a different estimate of inflation to the RPI through differences in the methodology, with the CPI usually producing a lower value than the RPI. The government considered the CPI to be a better measure than the RPI and changed the inflation target from the RPI to the CPI in 2003. This was seen as a technical change which didn't attract much attention from the general public; it didn't directly affect any payments the public received and even many economists seemed unconcerned by such a change. The situation was different in 2010, when the government changed the indexing measure for the state pension and for wage increases for public sector workers; further changes followed in the indexation of benefits. Having two competing measures led to disagreements over which was best; there is still a body of opinion that favours the RPI while there are those who argue that it represents a poorer measure of inflation.

These changes of inflation measure for indexation were part of a long-term government strategy to replace the RPI with the CPI, though initially, it was instances where the government paid out money which saw changes. Where the government generated income, the RPI was often left as the indexation measure. The declaration by the ONS that the RPI was no longer a good measure of inflation in 2012 led to the government accepting that there should be no new uses of the RPI and a gradual phasing out of its remaining uses. Chapter 6 covers the consultation on the RPI carried out by the ONS in 2012 and the Johnson Review in 2014–15 which together shaped the future for the measurement of inflation in consumer prices in the UK.

Changes to the longer-term applications of the indexing measure, such as to index-linked government bonds and private sector pensions, are more problematic. It was only in 2019, following a highly critical report from the House of Lords Economic Affairs Committee, that the UK Statistics Authority notified the Chancellor of the Exchequer of its intention to amend the methodology of the RPI to ensure the measure meets international standards. The implications of such a move are considerable and the Chancellor has insisted on a delay to at least 2025 and possibly extending until 2030. Chapter 7 describes the developments over the period from the 2012 consultation to the statement from the UK Statistics Authority and the response from the Chancellor.

1.6 The Wider Picture for Measuring Inflation in Consumer Prices

The scope of this book is the story of the RPI, an index which has greatly improved our knowledge of inflation, but has latterly lost its once prominent place. To tell the story effectively, the context in which events and developments took place has been covered, but only briefly. There is a wider picture which includes the whole of the current state of the measurement of inflation in consumer prices. While it is out of scope for this book, a brief description is given in this section.

The Harmonised Index of Consumer Prices was first produced in the UK in 1997 with the UK version named the Consumer Prices Index (CPI). When it was introduced, it was missing a component for the contribution of owner occupiers' housing costs. This was recognised as a major omission and a programme of work was put in place across European statistical organisations (including the ONS), to decide on the most appropriate way of measuring it. Of all the goods and services in an index of consumer prices, owner occupiers' housing is accepted as being the most difficult item to measure with a number of competing approaches having been proposed over the years. The RPI has included this item for some years, though the methodology it uses has been controversial.

A programme of study was put in place in the UK to decide on the best approach to use in incorporating a measure of owner-occupied housing in the CPI and a decision was reached in 2013; the UK would use the rental equivalence method (ONS 2018). This approach uses the notional changes in the cost of renting a property that a consumer owns. The RPI used this method initially but later changed to a user cost approach that included mortgage interest payments. For the purposes of comparison within the EU, a different approach was chosen by Eurostat (the statistical office of the European Union)—the net acquisitions method. This means that, for the UK version of the HICP, the ONS has to produce a measure of owner occupiers' housing cost inflation using the rental equivalence method for domestic use and another measure using the net acquisitions approach for European comparisons.

The Consumer Prices Index, including the rental equivalence measure of owner occupiers' housing, has become known as the CPIH; that is, the CPI including housing (ONS 2018). It is the ONS's preferred measure of inflation. It is expected that, in the near future, the government will switch uses of the CPI to the CPIH. The two indices are not usually far apart, so there will not be the same level of difficulty in implementing this change that has accompanied the switch from the RPI to the CPI.

1.7 The Longer Term and the Need for Stability

As Chaps. 5 and 6 explain, the period from 1990 to 2010 saw significant changes in the official statistics for measuring inflation in consumer prices. While it is important to make changes to ensure that official statistics are produced to the highest standard using the best methodology, large changes are difficult for many users. As noted in previous sections, those applications that have long-term needs are particularly affected by changes;

these include holders of index-linked government bonds, companies, trustees and beneficiaries of private pensions, and businesses entering into and servicing long-term commercial contracts.

Companies with pension schemes and pension trustees need to look to the long term in order to assess the liabilities of their schemes and to ensure that pension assets meet the liabilities. This is best achieved when inflation measures are subject only to minor changes, such as the update of the basket of goods and services. For these long-term applications, it would be beneficial if the CPIH retains its status as the preferred measure for the foreseeable future. We will have to wait and see whether a degree of stability over the long term is achieved, or if there are future changes in the area of inflation measurement.

While the CPIH has been developed from economic principles for official uses, the Royal Statistical Society (RSS) has been pressing for a new measure of inflation that is more suited to showing the inflation experiences of households—a household costs index. The benefits and broad conceptual principles were set out in a paper commissioned by the RSS in 2015 (Astin and Leyland 2015). The ONS has accepted the value of such a measure and is creating a family of such indices, using a different methodology to the CPIH in several respects; sets of experimental statistics have been produced both using the CPIH methodology and the household costs index methodology (ONS 2017, 2019b) which show varying inflation experiences for different population groups.

References

Astin, J., & Leyland, J. (2015). *Towards a household inflation index.* Retrieved May 15, 2020, from https://rss.org.uk/RSS/media/News-and-publications/Publications/Reports%20and%20guides/Astin-Leyland-HII-paper-Apr-2015.pdf

O'Neill, R., Ralph, J., & Smith, P. A. (2017). *Inflation: History and measurement.* Basingstoke: Palgrave Macmillan.

ONS. (2017). CPIH-consistent inflation rate estimates for UK household groups: 2005–2017. Retrieved December 16, 2019, from https://www.ons.gov.uk/economy/inflationandpriceindices/articles/cpihconsistentinflationrateestimatesforukhouseholdgroups20052017/2005to2017

ONS. (2018). *CPIH compendium.* Retrieved December 16, 2019, from https://www.ons.gov.uk/economy/inflationandpriceindices/articles/cpihcompendium/2016-10-13

ONS. (2019a). *Average weekly earnings in Great Britain: November 2019.* Retrieved December 16, 2019, from https://www.ons.gov.uk/employmentandlabourmarket/peopleinwork/employmentandemployeetypes/bulletins/averageweeklyearningsingreatbritain/november2019
ONS. (2019b). *Household cost indices, UK: Methodology for second preliminary estimates, 2005–2018.* Retrieved December 16, 2019, from https://www.ons.gov.uk/economy/inflationandpriceindices/methodologies/householdcostindicesukmethodologyforsecondpreliminaryestimates2005to2018

CHAPTER 2

The Early History of Inflation Measurement

Abstract This chapter tells the story of the early development of inflation measurement from the first considerations of a "price level" in 1707 to the introduction of the Interim Index of Retail Prices in 1947. The period up to 1880 was dominated by the work of visionary individuals whose insights laid the foundations of both theory and practice. The resources of the state were harnessed to produce the first official inflation measure in 1914—the Cost of Living Index. The first use of indexation for adjusting wages followed soon after. The Index was subject to political control during the Second World War and didn't reflect the public experience of price changes. As a result, it became discredited and a fresh start was needed after the War.

Keywords Value of money • Early inflation history • Household budgets • Price data • Wage indexation

2.1 The Big Picture

Before embarking on the story of the Retail Prices Index, it is worth summarising the current position; that is, setting out what had to be developed to get to the inflation measures we use today. We tend to take official statistics like the Retail Prices Index for granted; however, an enormous amount of work has gone into their development over an extended period of time.

J. Ralph et al., *The Retail Prices Index*,
https://doi.org/10.1007/978-3-030-46563-6_2

This development can usefully be put into six categories:

- The concepts behind the measurement
- The specification and collection of data
- The detailed methodology
- An organization responsible for collecting data, making calculations and publishing the outputs
- Governance procedures
- The uses of inflation measures

Each aspect has its own history and collectively they fit together to give the overall picture. In the main, we have chosen not to describe the development of each aspect separately; we believe the story is best told in a roughly chronological order, with the aspects intertwined. In a short book, a detailed exploration of all these aspects is not possible. A fuller description can be found in our previous book (O'Neill et al. 2017).

2.2 The Origins of Inflation Measurement

The observation that prices of goods change over time as a result of adverse weather or conflict has been known since the time of Hammurabi (around 2150 BC). Large increases in the prices of essential items presented particular problems for both rulers and subjects. Over the following centuries attempts were made to control prices but without much success (Schuettinger and Butler 1979). However, it is thought that no systematic effort was made to measure a general level of prices until the eighteenth century when it took specific practical problems to establish the concept of an "overall, average level of prices" or "the value of money", then to devise a way of measuring it.

Bishop William Fleetwood is credited with the first practical comparison of the value of money between two time periods, described in his book, Chronicon Precosium (1707). He wrote of his long term interest in the "course of prices" which he put to good use when presented with a challenge. A regulation at an Oxford college stipulated that fellows were not permitted to benefit from an annual income in excess of £5; this rule and the sum of money were specified in the year 1440. The Bishop was asked whether it was reasonable to apply the same money threshold in the year 1707 given that prices had increased significantly since 1440.

The Bishop approached the question by selecting four items relevant to fellows—Corn, Meat, Drink and Cloth and examined average prices of each item at the two time periods. He found that in all four cases, prices had increased by between 5 and 6 times between 1440 and 1700. This led him to the conclusion that the appropriate threshold amount for a fellowship should be between £25 and £30 in 1700. In modern terms, we would say that he had established a relevant basket of goods and found the ratio of the average of the prices in the two time periods. This indicated between a five—and six—fold increase in the "level of prices". While we might admire the Bishop for his important insight, it seems he didn't view it in the same way. His book contains an interesting comment on how his knowledge of prices might be perceived:

> .... as the World now goes, the greatest (though I will think not the best) Part of Readers would be rather apt to despise than commend the Pains that are taken in making collections of so mean Things as the price of Wheat and Oats, of Poultry, and such like Provisions ....

A similar exercise in comparing the "level of prices" was carried out by Nicolas Dutot in 1748; he compared the income of the French kings Louis VII and Louis XV, again selecting a "basket of goods and services". He was the first to produce an explicit formula for performing the calculation—the Dutot formula—the ratio of average prices[1].

The choice of formula is important, as we will see in later chapters—different formulas lead to different results (using the same data) when calculating the "level of prices". In 1764, an alternative formula was proposed by Rinaldo Carli, a professor of astronomy from Milan—this was the average of ratios of prices. In this formula, the ratio of the prices for each item in the two time periods is calculated and the average of these ratios is taken; it is known as the Carli formula after its originator. These two formulas are not just historical curiosities, as we will see in later chapters.

The work of Bishop Fleetwood and Nicholas Dutot in comparing prices between two time periods was important, but limited to a specific situation in each case. The credit for setting the "course of prices" in a more general context goes to Sir George Shuckburgh Evelyn. As well as being the MP for Warwickshire between 1780 and 1801, he was also a fellow of the Royal Society with interests in astronomy and the science of

[1] Appendix A contains the mathematical representations of this and other formulas.

measurement. In 1798, he published a paper on weights and measures—"An account of some endeavours to ascertain a standard of weight and measure" (Shuckburgh Evelyn 1798). This paper, comprising 23 pages, includes two pages at the end on a rather different topic—the way prices of various goods and services change over time, which was another of his interests. At the end of his paper, he presented the prices of a collection of items which included "wheat, horse, cow, goose, hen, butter, small beer and a day's labour", between the years 1050 and 1795. He combined these prices to give an estimate of the "level of prices" over this long time period. To give a clearer representation of the change over time, he set his level of prices to be 100 in 1550 and scaled the other values relative to the value at 1550. Today we recognise this as an index number representation—it seems a very modern touch. Table 2.1 shows his series of index numbers for the level of prices, using his terms as column titles.

In an echo of Bishop Fleetwood's comment on his study of the course of prices, Shuckburgh Evelyn writes:

> ... However, I may appear to descend below the dignity of philosophy in such economical researches, I trust I will find favour with the historian and the antiquary.

Table 2.1 Shuckburgh Evelyn's index of a combination of the prices of articles at different times

Year of our Lord	*Mean appreciation*
1050	26
1100	34
1150	43
1200	51
1250	60
1300	68
1350	77
1400	83
1450	88
1500	94
1550	100
1600	144
1650	188
1700	238
1750	314
1800	562

While the embarrassment felt by both Bishop William Fleetwood and Sir George Shuckburgh Evelyn in studying prices might appear to us to be a comical juxtaposition of the relative merits of (natural) philosophy and economics, there is an important point here. It was noted by several later commentators that it took a long time for the value of money to be studied seriously. At the same time, great efforts were made in scientific endeavours to estimate the distance to the sun and the weight of the atmosphere. While natural philosophy was recognised as being a noble subject to study, the practical benefits from a good quality measure of the level of prices was seriously under-appreciated with its potential to improve the lives of a great many people. But Shuckburgh Evelyn would be reassured to know that his researches have contributed to an important and widely-used branch of knowledge.

Although Shuckburgh Evelyn's work presents a step forward, with a "basket" containing both goods and services and extending the estimation of the level of prices over a long time period, his actual results were not given great credibility. The prices he used were not considered either representative or sufficient in quantity, so his results for the level of prices over time were disputed. The agriculturalist, Arthur Young (1812), criticised Shuckburgh Evelyn's work and created his own table of price changes introducing the multiple counting of items "which held greater importance", an early step towards the relative weighting of price changes (Young 1812).

While a number of individuals made important early contributions to establishing the measurement of inflation, the firm foundation of the study of the level of prices and index numbers is attributed to the Scottish political economist, Joseph Lowe. In his book, "The present state of England in regard to agriculture, trade and finance" (Lowe 1823), he explained clearly the tendency for prices to fluctuate, the impossibility of controlling prices and the benefits from having a robust measure "of the power of purchase" to enable compensation to account for "the injurious effects of price fluctuation":

> In what, it may be asked, would the benefits of it consist? .... It would correct a long list of anomalies in regard to rents, salaries, wages, etc. arising out of the unforeseen fluctuations of our currency.

He described the need for a more comprehensive basket of goods and services, divided into categories, with prices collected and proportions of expenditure determined, the latter providing weights. He explained clearly that despite the efforts of governments, price fluctuations were inevitable and it was through applying compensation payments linked to the level of prices that an effective accommodation could be made. It would take almost another century before this would be achieved.

2.3 Combining Prices and Expenditure Data

It is useful to pause at this point and identify the elements of the mechanism of inflation measurement that had been established by the time of Joseph Lowe, that is, around the 1830s. The concept of an "overall value of money" and an understanding that it changes over time were recognised together with the importance and usefulness of being able to calculate it. The calculation required the identification of a collection of goods and services which people consume (what we would term a representative "basket of goods and services"). Then both the prices of "basket items" and the proportions of expenditure spent on them needed to be recorded so that they could be combined together in a price measure. While Lowe understood that a much broader range of goods and services was needed, the substantial scale of the data collection that would be required for a robust measure was almost certainly not appreciated as it was so far outside the experience of contemporary statistical data collections.

The way that price and expenditure data for many goods and services should be combined together was another crucial question. What formula should be used? The two formulas proposed by Carli and Dutot contain only prices while the formula described by Joseph Lowe included weights to combine price changes. When calculating the overall price change, the proportion of household expenditure on an item should be included to reflect the relative importance of the change in price of that item. Although Lowe didn't write down such a formula, he described it sufficiently for it to be associated with him. The Lowe formula uses both prices and expenditure weights. It is the formula used in calculating the general level of prices by almost all statistical agencies around the world today. Appendix A contains the mathematical expressions for his and other formulas.

In the nineteenth century, many other experts contributed to the emerging field of index numbers and the estimation of the level of prices. Étienne Laspeyres, Herman Paasche and Mortiz Willhelm Drobisch all suggested alternative formulas for the change in the general level of prices.

Further formulas followed and efforts to identify a "best" formula have continued to the present day (Ralph et al. 2015).

Having established the key concepts and a formula to calculate the level of prices we turn our attention to the availability of price and household expenditure data.

2.4 Early Household Expenditure Data

We have seen that to produce a measure of the level of prices, it is not only the prices of goods and services that are needed. Arthur Young and then Joseph Lowe recognised that the proportion of household expenditure on goods and services was needed too. This section gives a brief history of the capture of expenditure data from households.

An early investigation into what was known as "household budgets" was carried out by William Petty in 1670 who proposed that society could be studied numerically through "political arithmetick"; he identified "typical workers" and constructed household budgets for each type. His work led him to conclude that the majority of the population lived in poverty, at least some of the time. In 1690, Gregory King took what sparse information was available on prices, wages and patterns of consumption to create "hypothetical budgets" for social classes based on "rank and title". Davies and Eden investigated the effect of bread price rises on agricultural labourers at the end of the eighteenth century; they were the first researchers to collect data directly from families. They found that three quarters of agricultural household income was spent on bread (O'Neill et al. 2017, pp. 197–198).

The work of the social reformers Seebohm Rowntree and Charles Booth at the end of the nineteenth century was particularly influential in advancing knowledge of household income and expenditure. They were concerned with estimating the extent of poverty and set out to interview every family in selected areas of the country; for Rowntree this was part of York and for Booth, parts of London. Both found that about 30% of families had barely adequate provision; this was ten times the official figures for "paupers". Although these investigations didn't seek to determine expenditure shares to incorporate into measures of the level of prices, they established the principle of estimating household expenditure by capturing data directly from households on a large scale (Kendall 1969).

Rowntree and Booth both knew that the expense of collecting data from every household in a given area would restrict their investigations.

However, an important step came when Arthur Bowley, a Professor of Statistics at the London School of Economics, showed that a carefully constructed sample of households was sufficient to obtain accurate data on household expenditure. He carried out a 1 in 20 sample collection of data from households in Reading in 1913; this is believed to be the first random sample survey in the UK (O'Neill et al. 2017, pp. 198–199).

The work of Rowntree, Booth and Bowley established the practice of capturing data from households and, through sampling, a practical method of doing so without the need to contact every household.

2.5 Early Price Series

It was in the nineteenth century that systematic attempts were first made to collect comparable price data over extended periods of time for a specified set of items. The Economist magazine published a price index for commodities from 1864 with data going back to 1845 based on 22 commodities. It is a very long running series which is still produced today. A more extensive source of data came from the German Chamber of Commerce which collected price (and quantity) data for 300 items from 1847. Note that these series were for wholesale prices; a consumer price index requires retail prices and these would only come later. Individuals were behind these early price series. In Germany, Adolf Soetbeer was the initial driver behind the Chamber of Commerce data, and in England a wool merchant, Augustus Sauerbeck, established price series of raw materials for the years 1848–85 (Balk 2008, p. 10).

These efforts by motivated individuals showed a clear understanding of the need for regular recording of prices for the purposes of detailed study. In a similar way, individuals drove the developments in capturing household expenditure data. Important though this was, they could not achieve the scale required to produce a national measure of the general level of prices—to move forward from this point required the resources of the state. It is an important juncture in our story. The history of measuring inflation is usefully divided into (roughly) the period 1700–1879 where the concepts and the basic methods were established by motivated and insightful individuals and 1880 onwards where state agencies took over the development and practice.

2.6 Better Statistics and the Political Debate

While the need for state involvement gradually became clear, it did not happen in a straightforward manner. A period of campaigning by individuals and organisations preceded the decision to enhance the Board of Trade's statistical capability (first established in 1832) to investigate the level of prices. It was also opposed by some parts of government. George Howell, a member of the TUC Parliamentary Committee, made representations to the government for the provision of labour statistics in 1869 without success. In 1879, he wrote an article in the Beehive magazine making the following point:

> ...the vast and daily importance of all movements connected with labour ...point conclusively to the necessity of a Bureau of Statistics of Labour, where the statesman, philanthropist, author, journalist or citizen, can at all times obtain authentic information and reliable statistics ....

A Treasury committee to enquire into the position of official statistics sat in 1879 and made positive statements but failed to lead to improvements in statistical capability. The Royal Statistical Society had been running a campaign for better labour statistics and in its jubilee year of 1885, the President, Sir Rawson Rawson, pressed the government for a reappraisal of social and industrial statistics to align with the more established position found in the US and other European countries (Davidson 1985, pp. 80–81).

Eventually, the political pressure for better data to inform parliamentary debate on a range of topics, including wages and the cost of living, did yield additional resources for the Board of Trade with the formation of firstly a Labour Section in 1886 and then a Labour Department in 1893—"... a refinement of the machinery of civil intelligence ...". However, this development was not appreciated by all parties. In fact, the context in which the Board of Trade's statistical work was carried out was a challenging one. Throughout the period 1886–1914, the Treasury opposed the expansion of statistical work, showing a clear disapproval of statistical investigation:

> .... the collecting and digesting of public statistics is a duty that should be carefully watched and guarded in order that it may not degenerate into extravagance. There is a dangerous tendency to magnify work and extend functions beyond the limits required at once by and expediency. (Davidson 1985, p. 169).

The Treasury opposed the appointment of professional statisticians who might counter their view that statistical enquiries were mechanical work appropriate only for junior administrators. The risk that allowing statistical enquiry might uncover justification for additional government expenditure was also a concern for Treasury officials (Davidson 1985, pp. 169–170).

Outside of government there were other avenues of resistance to the development of official statistics. Labour leaders were suspicious that enquiries into working-class expenditure and the cost of living would "obscure the fundamental causes of destitution" and provide an excuse for "middle-class moralising". Employers were also suspicious, believing that the work of the Labour Department on wages and household expenditure would intrude into what was a private matter between employers and their workers and threaten managerial autonomy (Davidson 1985, pp. 209–210).

Despite operating with limited resources and in a far from benign environment, the statisticians at the Board of Trade gradually put in place the essential ingredients of a measure of the level of prices. The period from 1886 saw the beginning of their work on household budget studies and the collection of wholesale prices. Their investigations were brought together quickly in 1903 following a specific request from the Prime Minister, Arthur Balfour, who asked for information on wages and the cost of living for Britain and competitor nations (Searle 2015, p. 147).

2.7 Early Official Price and Household Expenditure Data

Two important official documents on prices and household expenditure were delivered by the Board of Trade in August of 1903. The first, "A Report on Wholesale and Retail Prices in 1902 with Comparable Statistical Tables for a Series of Years" (Board of Trade 1903a) was the result of two years of work by the Labour Department on the course of prices in the UK covering wholesale prices for a range of goods and some retail prices. The inclusion of retail prices was significant; the document notes that "… so far as it is known this is the first attempt to compile continuous records of retail prices of commodities in the United Kingdom in an official report". It also noted that "retail prices are much less abundant than wholesale prices, and a considerable portion [of the retail prices in the document] represents original research" (Board of Trade 1903a, p. xiii).

While the publication of the "course of retail prices" clearly presented a step forward, it was still the case that these prices were taken from a variety of sources of limited quality. For wholesale prices, the sources included trade associations, markets, farmers' clubs, asylums and hospitals. For retail prices, which covered bread, other food commodities and a few non-food domestic items, prices were mostly for London only; the sources were firms, clubs and hotels, sometimes without a clear specification of quantities (Board of Trade 1903a, pp. 214–372). The report is also notable for its Appendix II "On the Construction of Index Numbers". This provided an overview of how index numbers are calculated and explained that the Labour Department had taken expert advice on the formula to be used to combine price series and weighting information (Board of Trade 1903a, pp. 426–451).

The second document—"British and Foreign trade and Industrial Conditions", contained data on the value of exports and imports from major trading partners, the course of money wages and the consumption of food by the working classes. Price information from the first document was combined with household budget data on food taken from an earlier US study in 1889. This source of expenditure data was chosen as it included expenditure on Germany as well as the UK giving a means to compare the outputs between the two countries. The combination of prices and expenditures yielded an early "cost of living" series for food for the UK which was set out in this second Board of Trade document. The series covered the period 1877 to 1901 and showed a fall from an index value of 143 in 1877 to 100 in 1901 (Board of Trade 1903b, chap. 18).

The limitations of both the household budget data collected by the Board and the US data were clear to the statisticians in the Board of Trade. Their enquiry was almost entirely based in London and very little data on non-food items was collected. A much more comprehensive survey on household expenditure was carried out in 1904, with better geographical coverage and extended to include rent, clothing and fuel. Further work was carried out in 1907 (Board of Trade 1905, 1908). With this data, an improved cost of living series was produced. This 1904 household budget survey would still be in use over forty years later.

While the extent and quality of price data was poor by modern standards, the work of the Board of Trade in the early years of the twentieth century shows clear progress towards a measure of the level of retail prices, with the beginnings of official data collection and the development of expertise in index numbers.

2.8 The First World War and the Cost of Living

Trade Boards were to play an important role in the early use of inflation measures. These boards were authorised through the Trade Board Act of 1909, introduced by Winston Churchill, then the president of the Board of Trade. Their aim was to determine legal minimum wages in industries with a tradition of low wages. The Trade Boards comprised a range of stakeholders drawn from employers, workers and civil servants. The Act became effective in January 1910, initially for four trades: tailoring, box making, machine-based lace finishing and chain making; the legislation allowed for other trades to be included later. Mining was added in 1912. By 1916, there were eight Trade Boards in Great Britain and five for Ireland covering minimum pay for half a million workers (Sells 1939, p. 22).

The effect of the onset of war on prices was seen almost immediately. The September report of the Board of Trade stated that food prices had risen 15% in the first eight days of the War, and although this rate of increase didn't persist, prices continued to rise. The rapid change in prices meant that regular reporting was required; previously the Board of Trade published limited information on retail prices from time to time. From July 1914, prices for a range of foods were published every month. With regular collection of prices and the data from the household budget survey from 1904, the Board of Trade created the first index of consumer prices—the Cost of Living Index, which aimed to cover the inflation experience of the working class. Table 2.2 shows the Cost of Living Index numbers for food only and also for all items covering the years 1914–19, with 1914 = 100.

Rapid price rises brought the potential for industrial unrest and presented a threat to the overall economic effort. To reduce the risk of industrial disruption, Trade Boards made adjustments to wages taking into account the Cost of Living Index. In addition to the existing Trade Boards, new wage-fixing tribunals were set up under the Munitions of War Acts of 1915. The definition of "munitions workers" was very broad and covered a large proportion of British workers (Sells 1939, p. 25). With the state of national emergency, pay was adjusted to accommodate price rises using bonuses or increments to base rates. In this way, the mechanism of adjusting rates of pay in line with the level of prices was first established.

Table 2.2 Cost of living index numbers for 1914 to 1919

Year	*Index numbers (1914 = 100)*	
	Food	*All items*
1914	100	100
1915	131	123
1916	160	146
1917	198	176
1918	215	203
1919	219	215

A further Trade Boards Act was passed in August of 1918, extending the scope of the original Act to include minimum wage setting for further industries. The minimum wage rates were revisited periodically to account for overall changes in price levels.

2.9 Between the Wars

A more direct link between wages and the cost of living was established after the War. Sliding scales were introduced which adjusted wages by set amounts in line with movements in the Cost of Living Index; this included reducing wages if prices fell. The first of these scales operated in 1919 for wool and worsted workers but quickly spread to railway workers, the police and other public sector workers. By 1922, it was estimated that three million workers were covered by these sliding scale agreements (Searle 2015, p. 150).

In the first few years of the 1920s, the Cost of Living Index fell sharply, from 249 in 1920 to 174 in 1923 (1914 = 100). It continued to fall and by 1925 the number of workers covered by sliding scales had reduced to 2.5 million—the reduction of wages due to a falling index made sliding scales unpopular. It wasn't just workers under these arrangements experiencing falling pay; the Ministry of Labour recorded wage reductions for more than 7 million workers. Although these reductions in wages were clearly undesirable to workers, this should be seen in context—many workers were put on short-time working or lost their jobs altogether (Burnett 1969, p. 310).

As wages fell, so the use of sliding scales continued to decline. By the 1930s, there were just 1.25 million workers in the schemes. The situation changed in 1934 when prices started to rise and Trades Unions pressed for wage rises (Searle 2015, p. 150). Despite the changing popularity of sliding scales, wage rates largely kept in line with the Cost of Living Index between 1914 and 1937 (Sells 1939, p. 376).

In addition to the linking of wages to the Cost of Living Index, the wider use of a measure of the level of prices began in the interwar period. A portion of civil service and armed forces pensions was linked to the Cost of Living Index and reference to the index was used to set levels of unemployment assistance. The combination of the linking of wage rates to the index, together with its wider use in "indexation", established the level of prices as a very important economic indicator (Searle 2015, p. 151).

After the War, household budget expenditure shares continued to be taken from the Board of Trade's 1904 survey. Through the 1920s, it was recognised that the spending patterns of households had changed; however, another budget survey wasn't carried out until 1937/38. To modern eyes, this seems extraordinary. Proposals were put forward for a new budget survey in 1926. Plans were drawn up for a survey of 5000 households and major stakeholders were consulted. The TUC objected on the basis that there were still restrictions in place from the War and the National Confederation of Employers Organisations (a forerunner of the current Confederation of British Industry) felt that the time was not right. Both parties were sensitive to the potential for an outcome that would affect their members adversely (Ward and Doggett 1991, p. 139).

The use of the 1904 budget shares continued until 1936, when the Minister of Labour proposed a new survey; this time all parties agreed and it was carried out in 1937/38, though the Second World War intervened before it could be adopted in the Cost of Living Index. The old 1904 budget data would continue to be used until the Second World War was over.

2.10 The Second World War

At the start of the war prices rose sharply, triggering a round of wage claims including one from mine workers. Mine owners were willing to raise wages but only if the extra cost could be recovered through higher prices. The government was concerned by this—it would increase the Cost of Living Index and drive further claims for higher pay, with the danger of creating an inflationary cycle. One option was to remove the link between pay and the index; however, this was rejected on the grounds that the link was now firmly established in workers' minds. Instead, the government decided to control prices. Subsidies were applied but only to items included in the index, other items would be allowed to increase in price (Searle 2015, pp. 156–157).

This approach was in contrast to the response of the UK government to the abnormal level of demand in the first half of the First World War. Then the policy was to let normal market forces operate with supplies bought at market prices. This resulted in prices rising sharply in the face of significant increases in demand leading to higher costs for the government. Having learned from this experience, the government chose direct intervention to control prices in the Second World War (Slater 2018, p. 166).

The policy of subsidizing only items in the Cost of Living Index and leaving others to rise led to a growing disparity between the "official figures" and the experiences of consumers. The combination of a lack of confidence in the index combined with the mounting cost of subsidies meant that urgent action was needed when the Second World War ended (Searle 2015, p. 159).

2.11 After the Second World War

At the end of the war, it was recognised widely that the old working-class Cost of Living Index, which began at the start of the First World War, was in urgent need of replacement. The expenditure profile of households, or the "basis" of the index as it was known at the time, still came from the original 1904 survey. It was clear to all interested parties that household expenditures had changed considerably over the preceding 50 years and this was confirmed by the pattern estimated from the expenditure survey carried out in 1937/38, but not implemented in the Cost of Living Index due to the onset of war. Table 2.3 shows the comparison of household expenditure weights from 1904 to 1937/38. The "not in index" component refers to items present in the index for 1937/38 but omitted from the 1904 index, which includes alcohol and tobacco.

During the war, the selection of items in the basket had been chosen so as to "control the level of prices" rather than reflect the changes in overall prices and there was widespread loss of confidence in the measure. Over three million workers were on "sliding scales", where pay was linked to

Table 2.3 Expenditure comparison between 1904 and 1937/38

Group of items	*Weights based on 1904 expenditure*	*Weights based on 1937/38 expenditure*
Food	60	40.1
Housing	16	12.7
Clothing	12	9.5
Fuel and light	8	7.6
Other items		
– In index	4	8.1
– Not in index	–	22.0
Total	100	100.0

changes in the Cost of Living Index and Trades Unions were pressing for a better measure.

While the need for a new index was clear, exactly how to construct it was not. An obvious and important first step would be to update the weighting information—the "basis" of the index; however, it was not clear how best to do this. There was also a desire to improve the index in other ways. The Minister of Labour and National Service decided to appoint an expert committee to advise him. The Cost of Living Advisory Committee was appointed on 8 August 1946 and held its first meeting in January 1947 (O'Neill et al. 2017, p. 134). Its overall remit was:

> .... to advise on the basis of the official cost-of-living index figure and on matters connected therewith.

One of the members of the committee, Professor Roy G. D. Allen, wrote an article for the Spectator Magazine in October 1946 (Allen 1946) explaining the options for the choice of "basis":

- A new expenditure survey could be carried out which would provide updated consumption patterns; while this would take two years to complete, it would ensure the most up to date weighting data was being used;
- The expenditure pattern from 1937/38 could be used without needing to wait for two years; however, it would not provide a measure of post-war expenditure; or
- The old "basis" from 1904 could continue to be used.

The third option was rejected as being unacceptable; the choice was between the first two. A significant factor against the first option was the fact that with shortages and rationing continuing, a new survey to establish the "current" expenditure pattern would rapidly become out of date as the supply of goods improved. The committee investigated whether consumption was changing by comparing retail sales for a selection of types of goods between 1946 and 1947—this showed significant changes, indicating that the time was not yet right for commissioning a new expenditure survey. Another factor was the limitation on public spending—there were competing requirements for scarce funding for government work at this time.

Although the 1937/38 consumption pattern was out of date, its use would present a considerable improvement over the old basis, so it was decided that the new index should start with the 1937/38 consumption pattern, until conditions stabilised.

The Cost of Living Advisory Committee also considered the need for a regular update of the consumption pattern, or weights, to ensure the new index would stay up to date. This was considered to be part of a longer term strategy and needed further consideration; hence the new index would be an interim index at first. The committee also recommended that the basket of goods be expanded and the way prices were collected should be reviewed and improved if necessary. A separate Technical Committee was formed to consider the detailed aspects of the proposed changes. Both groups acted under time pressure to enable a new index to be produced as quickly as possible—"in a matter of months" (O'Neill et al. 2017, pp. 137–138).

2.12 The Interim Index

The interim Index of Retail Prices was first produced in June 1947. It used the 1937/38 consumption pattern, with a basket with 80 food items (up from about 20 items used in the Cost of Living Index) and the number of clothing prices increased four times. Alcohol was included for the first time, as were some services.

Although the new index was a considerable improvement over the old Cost of Living Index, the use of pre-war weighting information led to it being criticised. It was believed that it wasn't adequately capturing recent price rises. With this in mind, the Minister of Labour and National Service re-convened the Advisory Committee to consider "... whether conditions were sufficiently stable to justify the holding of a full-scale budget enquiry". The re-convened committee first met on 7 February 1951 and met on six further occasions. As well as the question of a new budget survey, the committee was asked to consider whether the basket of goods and services was extensive enough to capture accurately the overall change in prices. The committee noted that four years had passed since the start of the interim index and there was hope that spending patterns had now settled. Despite that passage of time, changes were continuing which were expected to affect spending patterns. The committee had to balance the lack of stability with the growing pressure for a new enquiry. It concluded that a new survey should be held as soon as possible and plans devised for regular updates. On the question of whether the basket was sufficient, the committee recommended that the Technical Committee examine this question and a number of other aspects of the methodology (O'Neill et al. 2017, pp. 136–137).

The results of the new budget enquiry and the recommendations of the technical group would lead to the stopping of the interim index and the start of a replacement index—the Index of Retail Prices, which is discussed in the next chapter.

References

Allen, R. G. D. (1946, October 4). The cost-of-living index. *The Spectator*, 8–9

Balk, B. M. (2008). *Price and quantity index numbers.* Cambridge: Cambridge University Press.

Board of Trade. (1903a). *Report on wholesale and retail prices in the United Kingdom in 1902, with comparative statistical tables for a series of years.* London: His Majesty's Stationery Office.

Board of Trade. (1903b). *Memoranda, statistical tables and charts prepared in the Board of Trade with reference to various matters bearing on British and foreign trade and industrial conditions.* Cd. 1761. London: His Majesty's Stationery Office.

Board of Trade. (1905). *Second series of memoranda, statistical tables, and charts prepared in the Board of Trade with reference to various matters bearing on British and foreign trade and industrial conditions.* Cd. 2337. London: His Majesty's Stationery Office.

Board of Trade. (1908). *Cost of living of the working classes. Report of an enquiry by the Board of Trade into working class rents, housing and retail prices together with the standard rates of wages prevailing in certain occupations in the principal*

industrial towns of the United Kingdom. Cd. 3864. London: His Majesty's Stationery Office.
Burnett, J. (1969). *A history of the cost of living*. Harmondsworth and Middlesex: Penguin Books Ltd.
Davidson, R. (1985). *Whitehall and the labour problem in late-Victorian and Edwardian Britain*. Kent: Croom Helm Ltd.
Fleetwood, W. (1707). *Chronicon precosium, or an account of English money, the price of corn and other commodities for the last 600 years*. London: Charles Harper.
Kendall, M. G. (1969). Studies in the history of probability and statistics, XXI. The early history of index numbers. *Review of the International Statistical Institute, 37*, 1–12. https://doi.org/10.2307/1402090.
Lowe, J. (1823). *The present state of England with regard to agriculture, trade and finance: With a comparison of the prospects of England and France* (2nd ed.). London: Longman, Hurst, Rees, Orme & Brown.
O'Neill, R., Ralph, J., & Smith, P. A. (2017). *Inflation: History and measurement*. Basingstoke: Palgrave Macmillan.
Ralph, J., O'Neill, R., & Winton, J. (2015). *A practical introduction to index numbers*. Chichester: Wiley.
Schuettinger, R. L., & Butler, E. F. (1979). *Forty centuries of price and wages controls—How not to fight inflation*. Washington, DC: The Heritage Foundation.
Searle, R. (2015). Is there anything real about real wages? *The Economic History Review, 68*, 145–166.
Sells, D. (1939). *British Wage Boards*. Washington, DC: The Brookings Institution.
Shuckburgh Evelyn, G. (1798). An account of some endeavours to ascertain a standard of weight and measure. *Philosophical Transactions of the Royal Society of London, 88*, 133–182.
Slater, M. (2018). *The national debt*. London: C. Hurst & Co. Ltd.
Ward, R., & Doggett, T. (1991). *Keeping score*. London: Central Statistical Office.
Young, A. (1812). *An enquiry into the progressive value of money in England, as marked by the price of agricultural products; with observations upon Sir G Shuckburgh's table of appreciation*. London: Hatchard.

CHAPTER 3

The Launch of the Index of Retail Prices

Abstract This chapter describes the introduction of the Retail Prices Index (RPI) in 1956. The weights in the RPI were derived from a new *Enquiry into Household Expenditure*, and the survey methods are described. The quality of the outputs and the way that parts of the population were excluded is discussed. The RPI also involved expanded data collection, and the main collection mechanisms are presented, together with the approaches used for some of the more conceptually challenging products. The chapter concludes with an overview of the uses of the RPI up to the 1970s.

Keywords Expenditure survey • Updating weights • Price collection • Indexation

3.1 The New Household Expenditure Survey

Once the Cost of Living Advisory Committee had recommended that there should be a new budget (household expenditure) survey as soon as possible, preparations were put in place and the "Enquiry into household expenditure" was undertaken during January 1953 to January 1954. The necessity for a survey having been recognised some years earlier, there had been time for some preparatory work, and a consortium of government departments, led by the Central Statistical Office, had designed and undertaken a series of experiments (Kemsley and Nicholson 1960). These

J. Ralph et al., *The Retail Prices Index*,
https://doi.org/10.1007/978-3-030-46563-6_3

experiments covered issues such as the best ways to collect data on expenditure and income, how to encourage cooperation with the survey, and whether it was necessary to collect information from all the persons in a household to get a good impression of expenditure. Kemsley and Nicholson (1960) also set out the general principles which would underlie the survey design. The data collection covered the whole calendar year so that it would be relatively unaffected by seasonal variations in expenditure. There was some debate about whether the survey should cover only the parts of the population which would be used for the new index, that is, excluding the highest and lowest earners. But there were other uses of such information which could be realised for only a small additional cost, so the survey covered the whole population (O'Neill et al. 2017, section 6.5). This survey with full population coverage provided detailed information on the expenditure patterns of different groups of people, and allowed the Technical Committee supporting the Cost of Living Advisory Committee to investigate the different expenditure patterns. This was in contrast to the approach introduced in the interim index which was based on the expenditure patterns of working class and agricultural households only, as collected in the 1937–38 expenditure survey. The new data allowed the minority of households with appreciably different patterns to be excluded, to obtain a basket that would be suitable for the majority of the population. The resulting price index would then be able to be used for uprating and similar purposes in the general population.

The household expenditure survey covered a sample of 20,000 addresses, making it the largest such survey in the UK in the twentieth century. It was selected as a two-stage sample of addresses, and the large sample size was used in expectation that the response rate would be rather low (Ministry of Labour and National Service 1957; Gazeley et al. 2017).

In fact the level of cooperation with the survey was surprisingly high. The influence of government in the lives of ordinary citizens was quite pervasive, with many of the emergency provisions arising from the Second World War having been continued for some years afterwards (Dunton 2014), so there was some expectation that people would refuse to participate in reaction to this. But about 67% of households cooperated fully with the survey, which asked for detailed expenditure information for three weeks (the longest diary period covered by an official household expenditure survey in the UK). Some of the selected addresses were found to be bombed, or otherwise not occupied. The survey was administered by interviewers from the Government Social Survey and the Ministry of

Labour and National Service. Households were offered a £1 incentive for each member for participating, but this did not seem to be a prime motivator in many cases, and there were lots of examples of households going to a lot of trouble to gather accurate information in support of the survey (Dunton 2014). This may be attributable to a sense of communal purpose remaining after the war, and a sense that the evidence would be useful as a component of wage uprating, since many people's wages were still linked to the Interim Index of Retail Prices at this stage. The monetary incentive was however helpful on occasion, particularly in poorer households.

There were of course parts of the population which were not so ready to participate. The Ministry of Labour and National Service gathered evidence from the interviewers and regional offices (available in The National Archives, Dunton (2014)). These reports indicated the types of households which were not so eager to cooperate—particularly male wage earners, the elderly, and the self-employed—in which latter category farmers were singled out as particularly reluctant. These are all categories of people who were more suspicious of the motivation of the survey, considering that the government might use it as a way to check whether they were paying the correct income tax. The introduction to the survey was however at pains to explain that the responses would be treated anonymously, so that individual respondents would not be identifiable. The elderly were more likely to be confused by the use of several forms (see Gazeley et al. 2017 for a description), but could be very conscientious respondents once they had agreed to participate. There was also a general impression that (farmers notwithstanding) people in rural areas were more likely to cooperate with the survey than people in urban areas, a situation which persists in survey-taking in modern times.

Thanks to recent digitisation activity, the raw data underlying the 1953–54 survey are now available from the UK Data Archive (Gazeley et al. 2016). Using this information, Gazeley et al. (2017) were able to show that the impact of under-representation of the elderly in the survey is not likely to have had a large impact on poverty estimation, so we may surmise that its impact on the basket of expenditure was also not big.

Nevertheless, there was considerable academic discussion around the quality of the estimates deriving from the household expenditure survey. The Royal Statistical Society held a discussion meeting in which Prais (1958) presented information on the effect of the length of the recording period on the levels of recorded expenditure, using an example from Israel which demonstrated that there could be both fatigue from participating in the survey over long periods (although this implication is perhaps countered by the stories of the care which respondents generally took, as described by Dunton (2014)) and differential reporting of expenditure on different commodities. It was already known by comparison with other sources that expenditure on alcohol and tobacco was under-reported. The availability of tax revenue information allowed the level of this under-reporting to be determined and corrected, but in many cases there were no alternative data sources, so the possibility of differential reporting cast at least some doubt on the composition of the basket. Prais noted that less expenditure was reported by those participating for a shorter time than those reporting for a longer time, and that the effect was less for regularly bought items than for occasional purchases.

Further analyses (not obviously related to Prais's prompting) were forthcoming from the Government Social Survey, and these pointed to the same kinds of effects. Kemsley (1961) examined the differences between reporting in the three weeks of the household budget enquiry, and detected higher levels of expenditure in week 1 than in weeks 2 and 3, which were similar; it was not possible to say whether the truth was closer to one of these, or somewhere between. The detected pattern was general over many expenditure categories, but there were categories which showed different patterns (including "other foods", which suggests some fatigue from respondents in providing codable responses to the survey, so that more expenditure ended up in the "other" category in weeks 2 and 3). Similar first-week effects had been noted in experiments which tested different approaches to the design of a household expenditure survey (Kemsley and Nicholson 1960). But the effects of this differential nonresponse on the composition of the basket were beyond the computational resources of the time to work out.

3.1.1 Defining the Population with Typical Expenditure Patterns

From the beginning of the twentieth century, the Cost of Living Index and the Interim Index of Retail Prices both used expenditure information from surveys (which were not frequent, see Chap. 2). All of these expenditure surveys were designed to collect information about the pattern of spending of working class households. The restriction of scope to suitable households was achieved by distributing "forms of return" to workmen's organisations and co-operative societies (Board of Trade 1905, p. 3).

Therefore the weighting of the headline index made it appropriate for describing the inflation experienced by working class households. The new Retail Prices Index was, however, to have a wider coverage which would make it representative of the inflation experience of the majority of the population. The 1953–54 household expenditure survey included the whole population, and for the first time this provided the data from which patterns of expenditure across the whole income distribution could be assessed.

The Technical Committee supporting the Cost of Living Advisory Committee therefore examined different approaches to segmentation of expenditure patterns. At the upper end of the income distribution, they considered the income of the head of household to be a better indicator of the expenditure pattern than the total household income. This seems rather curious, but the implication (Ministry of Labour and National Service 1956, para 6) is that they examined this assertion and found it to be more satisfactory than using the total household income, which pooled some typical expenditure patterns with the untypical ones. They therefore proposed a threshold of £20 per week gross income of the head of household to define households with atypical expenditure patterns, while acknowledging that there was no obvious point where the characteristics changed. They found the atypical expenditure patterns to be both "different and more variable".

Neither the income of the head of household nor total household income was adequate for the lowest expenditures. The former was not a good indicator of total household expenditure at the bottom of the income distribution, and the latter did not distinguish adequately between households whose circumstances were different. To define unusual expenditure patterns the Technical Committee therefore used a definition based on the source of income—when three quarters or more came from pensions and related benefits, pensioner households would be excluded. The aggregate expenditure patterns of the subgroups thus created were reported in the publication of the report of the expenditure survey (Ministry of Labour and National Service 1957 and are shown in Table 3.1).

These were important deliberations, which set the principles of how the RPI weights would be constructed, not just the distribution that would be used, but also implicitly that weighting would be plutocratic (weighted according to expenditure, so households do not contribute equally). Once

Table 3.1 Expenditure distribution in broad expenditure categories of excluded high income and pensioner households, and included index households from the 1953–54 Enquiry into household expenditure

	High income households	*Pensioner households*			*Index households*
		One person	*Two person*	*All pensioner households*	
Food	21.4	39.2	41.2	40.6	34.4
Alcoholic drink	3.4	1.4	3.1	2.3	3.5
Tobacco	3.9	2.1	5.7	4.1	7.0
Housing	8.9	18.9	13.2	15.4	8.7
Fuel and light	3.8	13.8	9.9	11.5	5.2
Durable household goods	6.1	3.4	4.1	3.7	7.0
Clothing and footwear	17.3	5.3	7.6	6.9	11.4
Transport and vehicles	9.2	2.0	2.4	2.2	6.9
Miscellaneous goods	6.4	6.6	7.1	7.0	7.1
Services	19.6	7.3	5.8	6.4	8.7
Total	100.0	100.0	100.0	100.0	100.0

Recalculated from Ministry of Labour and National Service (1957) Table 48. NB there are some minor differences from the published summary distributions due to differences in the way the estimates have been rounded

these principles were in use they were correspondingly more difficult to change, since this would affect the continuity of the index.

3.1.2 Regular Updating of Expenditure

When the enquiry into household expenditure was put in place in 1953, some elements of rationing following the war had already been lifted, but food rationing was only in the process of being ended. The expenditure survey had been delayed already because there was concern that expenditure patterns were changing, but the Cost of Living Advisory Committee had concluded that there was unlikely to be any stability soon (Ministry of Labour and National Service 1951). So as well as recommending a full-scale household expenditure survey, it was natural to gather evidence which would allow expenditure patterns to be updated. Indeed this was already seen in the planning for the 1953–54 survey, which envisaged a regular survey (Kemsley and Nicholson 1960). This led to the institution of the Family Expenditure Survey (FES) in 1957. The FES was on a smaller scale—obtaining responses from around 3000 households per year, and with a two-week diary period. But it provided invaluable information for updating the basket of goods. The smaller sample size and the consequently larger sampling errors suggested the need for caution about allowing the weights to be updated from a single year's information, as this could cause spurious changes. So a three-year moving average was used, eventually changing to single year estimates for most products after the FES sample size was doubled in 1967 (O'Neill et al. 2017, section 6.12).

The methodological investigations which had underpinned and followed the Enquiry into household expenditure were important in helping to understand the design options and the properties of the estimates from the FES. Turner (1961) investigated variation between reporting in the two weeks of the FES diary, finding similar differences to those observed in the Enquiry into household expenditure by Kemsley (1961).

The upper gross income threshold was updated to £25 for 1957 and 1958 and £30 for 1960 (Ministry of Labour 1962). Eventually the head of household gross income threshold was changed to a whole-household income, following the report of the Retail Prices Index Advisory Committee[1] (Department of Employment 1986, section C), still excluding the top 4% of the distribution. This situation continues today (ONS 2019, section 2.6.4). The exclusions at the lower end of the income distribution continued with only pensioner households deriving at least three quarters of their income from pensions and benefits. Non-pensioner households deriving much of their income from benefits are included in the RPI weighting.

3.2 The New Index of Retail Prices

The basket and weights derived from the Enquiry into household expenditure made the final building block for the new index, and the Index of Retail Prices (later the Retail Prices Index) was first published in January

[1] The Cost of Living Advisory Committee was renamed the Retail Prices Advisory Committee in 1971.

1956. This finally produced an index where all the components were calculated from credible sources and methods, and did much to reduce the criticism which had dogged previous measurements of inflation (Searle 2015).

3.2.1 Not the Cost of Living

The new Index of Retail Prices was the first to have a published detailed methodological description—Ministry of Labour and National Service (1959)—a forerunner of the full methodological document eventually produced regularly (Baxter 1998; ONS 2019). One of the first points made in this description was that the index did not measure the *cost of living*—but rather, that component of the nebulous concept of 'cost of living' which is attributable to price changes. This was an important change of emphasis from the Cost of Living Index from the first half of the twentieth century. And the new index, following the lead from the interim index, was to cover "the whole field of goods and services over which households distribute their expenditure". Certain items were excluded, largely on the grounds that the service element was difficult to define, including income tax, savings and subscriptions. But there were supporting considerations, with some elements such as life insurance and pension fund payments regarded as deferred expenditure, insurance being seen as a transfer of purchasing power between sectors, and capital payments as more in the nature of investment than consumption. Some of these elements have been more formally excluded from the conceptual basis of the index since then—for example, income tax is not a payment over which a household has any control, so it is not regarded as a purchase (ILO et al. 2004, p. 19).

3.2.2 A Designed Index System

The RPI was the first index of consumer prices in the UK where all the components were designed for regular updating. Price collections had always been regular, as they were the basis of what the index was trying to measure. But from 1956 the expenditure patterns had also been brought up to date, and this was quickly followed by a regular annual updating based on the Family Expenditure Survey. It was only a little later, in 1962, that the basket was also updated on an annual cycle (O'Neill et al. 2017, p. 59).

3.3 Enhancing the Basket and Scope of the Index

The interim index had already expanded the range of prices that were collected as the basic data from which the index numbers would be calculated, but this was extended further for the new Index of Retail Prices. Prices for 350 different commodities and services were collected in 91 *sections*, aggregated into 10 *groups*. These groups, together with their weights in parts per thousand in the index, were

I.	Food	350
II.	Alcoholic drink	71
III.	Tobacco	80
IV.	Housing	87
V.	Fuel and light	55
VI.	Durable household goods	66
VII.	Clothing and footwear	106
VIII.	Transport and vehicles	68
IX.	Miscellaneous goods	59
X.	Services	58

3.3.1 Price Collection

Several types of commodities had consistent pricing which could be collected directly from producers without the need for detailed collection. Tobacco prices were obtained directly from the manufacturers, with only some local collection where prices were considered to vary. Rent for local authority controlled accommodation, and rates (local taxes) were both obtained directly from Local Authorities. Gas and electricity prices were collected based on the tariffs of the suppliers and stylised consumption patterns for different types of household. Rail fares were obtained from the British Transport Commission, and transport prices in London from the London Transport Executive.

As well as these "central" collections there were two principal approaches to price collection. For the majority of foodstuffs and a few other commodities such as coal and cinema tickets, prices were collected by employees of the Ministry of Labour and National Service local offices, who would go out and identify the prices for defined products in the chosen outlets—which were determined by the managers in those offices. It was considered more important to have high quality price information from a sample of locations, rather than a larger quantity of price data, so a sample of 200 areas was chosen, covering London, and towns of varying sizes. The list of locations is given in Ministry of Labour and National Service (1959, Appendix C)—in contrast to modern practice that the locations from which prices are collected are not advertised. Where possible, five outlets were visited for each commodity within these localities. Durable goods were also collected this way, but from a smaller sample of retailers in large urban areas.

For a range of other commodities, including furniture, soft furnishings, hardware, clothing and bus fares, prices were collected through a postal survey addressed to a sample of retailers and service providers. Initially these retailers were visited by staff from the Ministry of Labour & National Service, and there were still occasional visits to answer queries, and to ensure that the prices were provided for products of consistent quality, so that the index would not be affected by quality changes.

3.3.2 Price Definition Challenges

In some commodities it was difficult to define the appropriate price to measure. Although alcoholic drink had already been added to the interim index, there were very real challenges over how to measure the price of beer, which formed the major part of the weight of group II. In principle a quality adjustment was needed so that the price referred to a product of consistent quality, and there were regular changes in the alcohol content of the beer, sometimes connected to price changes and sometimes not. But the quality of a pint was judged to depend on other attributes as well as the alcohol content, so the Cost Living Advisory Committee suggested taking the arithmetic average of the changes accounting and not accounting for differences in alcohol content. Effectively this took on half of the alcohol content changes as the measureable part of the quality change. But a large number of price quotes for different beers was needed in this category to deal with the variation in beers.

In the case of milk (in group I), there were several types of market in operation—some was provided free to schools (though presumably it was funded centrally—but such an arrangement would contribute to the wholesale price rather than the retail price). There were also some subsidised prices. So the price change was constructed as a weighted average of these three markets (including a zero price for 'free' provision).

At this time fruit and vegetable production was much more seasonal than today. A quality adjustment was made for potatoes, to account for the higher quality of new potatoes; this was a simple scaling adjustment that said that a smaller weight of new potatoes was equivalent in quality to a fixed weight of potatoes at other times. The Technical Committee also considered whether there should be seasonal weighting to cope with seasonally available fruit and vegetables, but this made only a small difference in the index, and would have been a complicated process. It was therefore rejected. Indeed, most of the price quotes among fruit and vegetables were for items which were available all year round, which was part of the criteria for their selection. However, there was an adjustment in the *Other vegetables* category to deal with a few items in the periods when they were unavailable. In months when no price could be obtained, the weight for these items was distributed over the other price quotes in this part of the index.

3.3.3 Owner Occupiers' Housing Costs

Defining prices in some components of a price index is conceptually challenging, and there are some topics which have been persistently the topic of research and debate through the life of the different measures of inflation. This was also true as the RPI was brought into being, and one of the important topics was how to measure owner occupiers' housing costs. The general approach was one of rental equivalence—imputing the rent that an owner occupier would need to pay to rent their own home. This element was included in the weights for housing (group IV) by using the gross values of the dwellings on Schedule A of the rateable values system, with some uprating to account for increases in prices since the last reassessment of rateable values. This element was therefore included in the basket and the weight for housing. Gathering price information to support this approach was however too challenging, and therefore the weight was distributed across the other elements of the housing component—rent, rates, repairs & maintenance and home repair & decoration. This seems likely to have increased the weight on rents for lower-value properties relative to more expensive (owner occupied) properties, but as long as the increases were in line in the two types then may have been a reasonable approximation. However, allocating part of the weight to repairs and maintenance activities seems likely to have misrepresented changes in the owner occupier element and the weight was moved wholly to the rent series following the advice of the Advisory Committee (Ministry of Labour 1962). Chapter 4 describes the difficulty in measuring this good more fully.

3.3.4 Meals Out

Another topic that has persistently exercised price statisticians is how to measure the costs of meals taken outside the home. At the beginning of the RPI the challenges posed were too difficult, and a pragmatic solution was adopted. The expenditure on meals out was available from the Enquiry into household expenditure, and this was split into two equal parts. One was assumed to represent the element from changes in food prices, and was therefore distributed proportionally to the food category (group I); the other represented elements of service and experience for which there was no suitable price source, so the weight was distributed across the whole of the remainder of the RPI, as the best available proxy.

3.3.5 Uncollected Prices

The weights for owner occupiers' housing costs and meals out were updated through the expenditure survey, but there was no suitable source of price information. Both of these would be revisited later by the Cost of Living Advisory Committee (see Chap. 4), and eventually suitable price collections would be added. Some other smaller items were not included in price collections at the inception of the RPI, including holiday expenditure, education and hobbies, and the weights for these were similarly distributed across the whole of the remainder of the index.

3.3.6 Elementary Aggregates

At the lowest level of the index, different approaches were used to combine the prices to make elementary aggregate indices (Ministry of Labour and National Service 1959). For most of the food product group and some other products where prices were collected by Ministry staff, prices were averaged within towns and then combined to form an index—therefore using the Dutot formula for elementary aggregates (see Sect. 4.2 and Appendix A for more about elementary aggregate formulas). For a few such products, and for products where prices were obtained centrally (by postal collection), price relatives were calculated first and then averaged—therefore using the Carli formula. In both cases these elementary aggregates were further aggregated using unweighted averages, because the detailed weighting information to combine the indices was not available.

3.4 A Period of Stability

The introduction of the Index of Retail Prices in January 1956 gave a new stability in the measurement of inflation in the UK. There was some consolidation in the methods, with changes to annual updating of the basket, and considerable work to evaluate the quality of the expenditure information on which the series was based. Regular annual updating of the weights was put in place (Ministry of Labour 1962), and extended to annual updating of the basket. But there were no major methodological or procedural changes for a number of years, and it was not until 1967 that the Cost of Living Advisory Committee would be commissioned to review the methods for some of the more challenging price measurements.

3.5 Uses of the Retail Prices Index

The most prominent political driver for the change to the Interim Index of Retail Prices was the use of its predecessor, the Cost of Living Index in sliding scale indexation agreements for the wages of a large number of manual workers (see Sects. 2.9 and 2.10). By 1944 around 2½ million workers were covered by these agreements (Goodman and Thomson 1973). The government's policy of subsidising products included in the index, and the use of very outdated expenditure patterns both led to dissatisfaction. Particularly, any inadequacy in the index would have a direct effect on the money in people's pockets, and this focussed opinions strongly (as it still does today, see Chap. 7). The interim index was clearly an improvement, although it did not satisfy all the dissent, and continuing questions about its quality eventually led to the Retail Prices Index.

There was naturally some hesitation at the time the Interim Index was introduced, and the sliding scales were suspended in some industries. But as the index established credibility the indexation was largely reintroduced where it had been stopped. By 1952, around 2 million workers were covered by these agreements, and there was essentially no change in this number with the introduction of the Retail Prices Index. The indexation was only a component of the change in wages, generally forming between 5 and 10% of the change during 1952–66, though forming almost 20% of the change in two years during this period (Goodman and Thomson 1973). In the late 1960s government policy turned against the use of indexation for wage agreements, and a National Board for Prices and Incomes was set up (McKersie 1967). Although this wasn't the only factor in play, the number of workers covered by such agreements fell rapidly, to around 150,000 in 1970. Goodman and Thomson (1973, Appendix A) give a list of agreements which were known to have included indexation at some stage after the First World War.

There was a brief return to larger scale indexation in 1973 when threshold agreements were introduced, to protect against high rates of inflation by increasing wages automatically when inflation breached a preset threshold (Braun 1976). This did not work well, partly because the additional wages were additive and eroded pay differentials, and partly because inflation was high and this quickly led to a feedback loop between wages and prices which undermined efforts to control inflation.

Outside wage agreements the use of the RPI was much less formal. Indexation of pensions was largely linked to increases in wages during the 1950s and 1960s, but not by any automated or legal mechanism (Wilson and Wilson 1982 in Vording and Goudswaard 1997). However, in 1973 a link to prices was established for state pensions and benefits, although the actual index to be used is not defined in the legislation (Vording and Goudswaard 1997). Since then there have been variations in the way that indices have been calculated or forecast, and there have been periods when there has been an additional linkage to wages, but the RPI has generally been used in indexation of pensions and benefits. A summary of the indexation changes since 1974 can be found in Department for Work & Pensions (2018, section 1).

References

Baxter, M. (Ed.). (1998). *The retail prices index technical manual.* London: Government Statistical Service.

Board of Trade. (1905). *Second series of memoranda, statistical tables, and charts prepared in the Board of Trade with reference to various matters bearing on British and foreign trade and industrial conditions.* Cd. 2337. London: His Majesty's Stationery Office.

Braun, A. R. (1976). Indexation of wages and salaries in developed economies. *Staff Papers (International Monetary Fund), 23*, 226–271.

Department for Work & Pensions. (2018). The annual abstract of statistics for benefits, and indices of prices and earnings. Retrieved February 29, 2020, from https://assets.publishing.service.gov.uk/government/uploads/system/uploads/attachment_data/file/672880/abstract-of-statistics-2017.pdf.

Department of Employment. (1986). *Methodological issues affecting the retail prices index. Cmnd. 9848.* London: HMSO.

Dunton, M. (2014). *Public cooperation with the Household Expenditure Enquiry, 1953–1954.* The National Archives podcast. Retrieved January 2, 2020, from https://media.nationalarchives.gov.uk/index.php/public-cooperation-household-expenditure-enquiry/.

Gazeley, I., Gutierrez Rufrancos, H., Newell, A., Reynolds, K., & Searle, R. (2017). The poor and the poorest, 50 years on: Evidence from British Household Expenditure Surveys of the 1950s and 1960s. *Journal of the Royal Statistical Society, Series A, 180*, 455–474.

Gazeley, I., Newell, A., Hawkins, M., Walker, J., & Scott, P. (2016). *Living standards of working households in Britain, 1904–1954.* [data collection]. UK Data Service. SN: 7916. https://doi.org/10.5255/UKDA-SN-7916-1.

Goodman, J. F. B., & Thomson, G. M. (1973). 'Cost of living' indexation agreements in post-war British collective bargaining. *British Journal of Industrial Relations, 11*, 181–210.

ILO, IMF, OECD, UNECE, Eurostat & The World Bank. (2004). Consumer price index manual. Geneva: International Labour Office. Retrieved March 1, 2020, from http://www.ilo.org/wcmsp5/groups/public/%2D%2D-dgreports/%2D%2D-stat/documents/presentation/wcms_331153.pdf

Kemsley, W. F. F. (1961). The household expenditure enquiry of the Ministry of Labour: Variability in the 1953–54 enquiry. *Applied Statistics, 10*, 117–135.

Kemsley, W. F. F., & Nicholson, J. L. (1960). Some experiments in methods of conducting family expenditure surveys. *Journal of the Royal Statistical Society, Series A, 123*, 307–328.

McKersie, R. B. (1967). The British Board for prices and incomes. *Industrial Relations, 6*, 267–284.

Ministry of Labour. (1962). *Report on Revision of the Index of Retail Prices.* Cmnd. 1657. London: Her Majesty's Stationery Office.

Ministry of Labour and National Service. (1951). *Interim report of the Cost of Living Advisory Committee.* Cmnd. 1657. London: Her Majesty's Stationery Office.

Ministry of Labour and National Service. (1956). *Report on Proposals for a New Index of Retail Prices.* Cmnd. 9710. Her Majesty's Stationery Office.

Ministry of Labour and National Service. (1957). *Report of an enquiry into Household Expenditure in 1953-4.* London: Her Majesty's Stationery Office.

Ministry of Labour and National Service. (1959). *Method of construction and calculation of the Index of Retail Prices* (2nd ed.). London: Her Majesty's Stationery Office.

O'Neill, R., Ralph, J., & Smith, P. A. (2017). *Inflation: History and measurement*. Basingstoke: Palgrave Macmillan. https://doi.org/10.1007/978-3-319-64125-6.

ONS. (2019). Consumer Prices Indices technical manual, 2019. Retrieved March 1, 2020, from https://www.ons.gov.uk/economy/inflationandpriceindices/methodologies/consumerpricesindicestechnicalmanual2019

Prais, S. J. (1958). Some problems in the measurement of price changes with special reference to the cost of living. *Journal of the Royal Statistical Society, Series A, 121*, 312–332.

Searle, R. (2015). Is there anything real about real wages? A history of the official British cost of living index, 1914–62. *Economic History Review, 68*, 145–166.

Turner, R. (1961). Inter-week variations in expenditure recorded during a two-week survey of family expenditure. *Applied Statistics, 10*, 136–146.

Vording, H., & Goudswaard, K. (1997). Indexation of public pension benefits on a legal basis: Some experiences in European countries. *International Social Security Review, 50*, 31–44.

CHAPTER 4

Improving the Index

Abstract In this chapter we examine the series of changes which have been made to the Retail Prices Index (RPI) over its life with the express aim of improving the ability of the index to measure changes in the general level of prices. These included changes in the statistical concepts underpinning the index, for example in dealing with issues such as owner-occupied housing, and practical concerns, such as how price collectors should behave when collecting information on items as varied and idiosyncratic as fashionable clothing. This chapter summarises the ways in which changes to the methodology of the index have sought to improve the ability of the index to reflect consumers' experiences.

Keywords Formula effect • Local price collection • Clothing prices • Owner occupiers' housing • Hedonics

Following the establishment of the RPI in 1956, a period of stability followed before its methodology underwent periodic development starting in 1962. The Advisory Committee was convened from time to time to consider specific issues and their recommendations were taken forward by the statisticians responsible for producing the RPI. As was noted in Chap. 3 (Sect. 3.3.3), a number of issues were discussed many times over the years as the index was developed and improved; this repeated consideration

J. Ralph et al., *The Retail Prices Index*,
https://doi.org/10.1007/978-3-030-46563-6_4

resulted from regular reviews of the effectiveness of the methodology, changes in user needs and changes in the consumer marketplace.

Another reason for revisiting the treatment of specific items is that some are very hard to measure effectively and their treatment needs to be reconsidered regularly. Fortunately, there are few of these items but they are important. For most goods and services, there is little change in their physical properties over time. Typical examples are basic commodities like bread and milk, and in addition, their prices are readily available from retail outlets. In this Chapter we consider more complex items and the ways in which the RPI and associated indices have been developed to include them in the measurement of overall price change in a more fluid consumer environment. We will consider what happens as technological improvements result in items that change rapidly (personal computers, mobile phones), or where services are not easily priced or understood (owner-occupiers' housing) and where the item contains a large fashion element (clothing).

The item considered to be the most challenging to include in an inflation measure is owner occupiers' housing. It was discussed by the Advisory Committee in 1952, 1962, 1968 and 1974. When the Harmonised Index of Consumer Prices was introduced in 1996 it was missing owner occupiers' housing and it took many years of discussion before decisions were made on how best to include it. Measuring inflation for two other types of item is also challenging: clothing and technological goods. Both have merited much expert consideration over the years.

4.1 Developing the RPI

The Advisory Committee spent a lot of time considering the best way to include these difficult items in the RPI, while it also provided advice on the treatment of many less complex items and debated a range of other issues. This section gives an overview of the developments that took place up to 1996.

In the 1960s, the Advisory Committee considered meals bought and consumed outside of the home, price indices for regions and for income and social groups as well as owner occupiers' housing. Meals out were a growing area of consumer expenditure and were given a more prominent position in the categorisation of goods and services with a dedicated group in the index, starting from 1968. An important change to the way expenditure weights were incorporated into the index was made in 1962—this saw the annual updating of the weights (see Sect. 3.1.2). The practicality of producing measures of inflation for regions had been first discussed in 1951 and it was considered again in the 1960s. Although the Advisory Committee believed it was possible to produce such measures, there were doubts over their usefulness and although there was a proposal to produce them, they didn't go ahead. In a similar way, inflation measures for social and income groups were considered. They weren't seen as sufficiently valuable, apart from a specific index for pensioners. In 1968, the Advisory Committee asked the RPI production team to produce a retrospective pensioner index for the period 1962–68 by using expenditure weights relevant to pensioner households. This showed an increase in prices of 26.0% against an increase of 21.9% for the main Retail Prices Index (Department of Employment and Productivity 1968). Two new indices were published quarterly from 1969, one for one-person pensioner households and the other for two-person pensioner households.

In the 1970s, the Advisory Committee revisited owner occupiers' housing, recommending a change in the way it was measured in the index from the existing rental equivalence method to a method involving mortgage interest rates. This is described more fully in Sect. 4.6. The introduction of mortgage interest rates led to the need for a variant which excluded them, RPIX, which was introduced in 1975. The treatment of rent rebates and seasonal food were also considered at this time (Department of Employment 1975). Another extremely important topic was first studied in the 1970s—the choice of formula at the lowest level of a consumer price index. This technical consideration became a crucial issue in the 1990s and beyond—it is discussed in the next section. The end of the 1970s saw a further variant of the RPI introduced—the Tax and Price Index. This index was an inflation measure that remained unaffected by movements between direct and indirect taxes. It was introduced after the government reduced income tax, which didn't affect the RPI, but raised VAT, which did.

The 1980s saw yet one more variant introduced. The Rossi index was used to uprate income related benefits; it excluded most of the housing sections of the RPI as recipients of these benefits were not expected to be paying significant housing costs. In 1983/84, UK and foreign holidays were included in the index and in 1986 a major restructuring of the bespoke classification of goods and services was made. This saw "durable household goods" and "miscellaneous goods and services" put into five new groups.

The period 1989–93 saw changes in the way taxes were raised for local government. The system of "rates" where local tax was levied based on a notional rental value of a house was replaced by the Community Charge in Scotland at the start of the 1989/90 financial year and in England and Wales at the start of the 1990/91 financial year. The Community Charge was levied as a flat rate per person with a discount for those on low incomes. This means of funding local government proved very unpopular and was replaced by the Council Tax system from the start of the 1993/94 financial year. Council tax was similar to the old rating system except that it was levied in a series of bands based on the capital value of a property rather than a notional rent. The RPI was changed to reflect the different local taxation approaches. The 1990s saw further changes, including the introduction of package holidays abroad and holiday insurance (O'Neill et al. 2017, pp. 153–155).

This section has summarised a wide range of developments of the RPI that took place in the period 1967–96. The next sections look at developments in specific areas that were either challenging or influential.

4.2 The Formula Effect

It is a curious feature of the story of the RPI that an obscure aspect of the technical methodology of inflation measurement became well-known and debated in the public arena. It concerned the formula used at the lowest level of the RPI—known as the elementary aggregate level. All indices of consumer price are constructed using hierarchical classification schemes. For the RPI, the top level is the whole index; this is divided into groups, such as "Food and Catering", then into sub-groups, such as "Food" and sections such as "Bread". The elementary aggregate level sits below this; an example of an elementary aggregate (or stratum) is "white sliced bread bought in an independent store in the south east of England". At this level of detail, weighting information is not usually available, so the price information is combined without weights. There is a variety of formulas that can be used and the RPI uses two that were introduced in Chap. 2: the Dutot and the Carli; Appendix A gives their mathematical forms. The Dutot formula is the ratio of the average of prices at the current period to the average of prices in the reference period. The Carli is the average of price relatives; that is, the average of price relatives where a price relative is the ratio of the price of an item in the current period to the price in the reference period.

In the early years of the RPI, price quotations were combined using both the ratio of averages and the average of ratios as described in Chap. 3 (Sect. 3.3.6). When the calculation of the RPI was computerised in 1966, the average of price relatives was used at all stages of the calculation (Carruthers et al. 1980).

Average prices for a range of goods were published regularly in the Department of Employment Gazette and it was noticed in the mid-1970s that, in some cases, price changes based on these average prices (using the Dutot formula) differed to price changes based on the average of relatives used in the RPI (using the Carli formula). These differences and the relative merits of the two formulas were studied in 1976 (Department of Employment 1976). This work showed that in most cases, the difference between formulas was small; however, in a few cases, the differences were significant, particularly over a run of several years. In order to decide which formula to use, the RPI production team in the Department of Employment studied the properties and behaviours, that is the differences between formulas in different price change scenarios. The Carli was long known to have some undesirable properties in certain situations (the lack of transitivity and the potential for chain drift, see Ralph et al. 2015). It was concluded that the Dutot was the preferred formula.

As this issue of which formula to use was a technical matter, it was not thought appropriate to reconvene the Advisory Committee to consider it, which usually discussed issues with a greater public aspect. Instead, it was discussed by the RPI Technical Committee, which was a specialist group convened to advise the Advisory Committee on technical issues. This group comprised Department of Employment specialists in the RPI and two external academic experts, Professor Sir Roy G. D. Allen and Professor Alfred R. Illersic. This group held a number of meetings and agreed that the Dutot should be used instead of the Carli. Other work carried out in early 1977 showed that improved item indices resulted from a new stratification scheme based on the form of the retail organisation and geography (Department of Employment 1977a; Carruthers et al. 1980).

The RPI Advisory Committee met on 24 November 1977 to discuss two issues:

- A proposal to publish more detailed section indices to one decimal place

- That certain technical improvements be made; these included the revised stratification scheme (stratification by region and shop type) and the change of (elementary aggregate) formula

The minutes of the meeting note that the Dutot formula was preferred: "the weight of theoretical argument was in favour of the ratio of averages formula" (Department of Employment 1977b). While the initial recommendation had been for the Carli to be replaced everywhere, the final recommendation for its replacement was for homogeneous items only; "other considerations" would apply for non-homogeneous items, though these other considerations weren't specified in the documentation (Carruthers et al. 1980). The changes were introduced in early 1978.

While the RPI underwent a significant revision in the mid-1980s, the records do not indicate any further work on the elementary aggregate formula question until the latter years of the 1990s. In the 1990s, three events provided motivation for a fresh look at the methodology of the RPI—a review of the RPI from the National Audit Office, a report from the Boskin Commission in the US and the introduction of a European measure of consumer price inflation—the Harmonised Index of Consumer Prices. In response, the RPI team instigated a methods research programme towards the end of 1998 extending to the year 2001, comprising ten separate projects. This work examined several aspects of the methodology, not just the formula effect issue (Baxter and Camus 1998).

The choice of elementary aggregate formula was a topic for this research programme and the work concluded that the Carli should not be used. However, this recommendation was not taken forward. Instead, a new method was devised to decide between the Carli and Dutot based on the variance of price quotes. For each stratum, the variance was calculated; if it was less than five, the Dutot formula was to be used. If it exceeded 20, the Carli was to be used. In between, the formula used in the rest of the section was chosen. Applying these rules led to 47 instances where the Carli was changed to the Dutot and one the other way round. The issue of the formula was examined again in 2005 and this work also concluded that the Carli should not be used; however, as before this was not taken forward (ONS 2012).

4.3 Price Collection at the Local Level

The extent and quality of the data used in the construction of a consumer price index are vital elements. As Chap. 2 explained, the early efforts were hampered by the lack of sufficient data and producing a robust national measure was not possible. By the time the RPI began in 1956, data collection had been established on a suitable scale, though the quality of price data was below the standards we are used to today. From the time of the old Cost of Living Index, which started in 1914, prices of many goods and services were collected by staff from local labour exchanges (see Sect. 3.3.1).

The system was largely the same in 1990 though it was the 175 Unemployment Benefit Offices and five parts of the Northern Ireland Department of Service and Personnel that provided the staff for local price collection. In contrast, some prices continued to be collected centrally, mainly goods and services whose prices did not vary across the UK, an example being newspapers. Central prices represented about 40% of the basket (by expenditure weight). As local price collection was the major component, its quality was a significant factor in the overall accuracy of the index. The methodology and practice of collection had potentially wide ranging implications.

In December 1987, the government informed the House of Commons that the RPI had understated consumer price inflation by 0.1% between February 1986 and October 1987. As a result, compensation payments totalling £118 million were paid to recipients of pensions and benefits. Given the scale of the implications of errors and inaccuracies in the RPI, the National Audit Office "examined the arrangements for compiling and updating the RPI" in 1989, reporting in February 1990. During the course of the enquiry, the responsibility for RPI was transferred from the Department of Employment to the newly expanded Central Statistical Office, reporting to Treasury Ministers; this took place on 31 July 1989 (NAO 1990).

One of the topics investigated by the National Audit Office was local price collection. Their report made clear that the practices of local price collection suffered from a number of problems. The main issue identified was the lack of standardisation across offices; the methods for price collection varied from office to office, there wasn't always evidence that all price quotes were in accordance with the guidance given by the central RPI team, there was high staff turnover and a lack of training and management supervision. It was noted that the staff responsible for the collection of the price quotes had other pressing concerns, notably the administration of unemployment benefits and mostly had little or no background in statistics and may even not have understood the importance of the data they were collecting.

Following the NAO's report, it was clear that there was an urgent need to change the way in which prices were collected for the RPI. When the responsibility for producing the RPI was transferred to the Central Statistical Office, the new owner instigated its own review with an exploration of possible alternative arrangements, and this led to the price collection being outsourced. The RPI Advisory Committee discussed the NAO report and published their views in the Committee report of July 1990. They agreed with the NAO findings, stating that "outdated arrangements had been allowed to continue for far too long and a thorough overhaul is now called for" (CSO 1990). This led to local price collection being contracted out to a private sector company specialising in data collection. The process was improved to include stringent supervision and quality checking. Allen (2017) gives some guide to the personal experience of a modern Price Collector and the way in which they work in order to collect a number of prices on Index Day each month.

4.4 The Treatment of Clothing

When the RPI was officially introduced in 1956, clothing and footwear accounted for 10.6% of the weight in the index. This has steadily declined and the category accounted for only 3.9% of the index weight in 2019 (ONS 2019a). Despite this steady decline in the proportion of spending devoted to clothing, the difficulties it has caused have increased over time, and in recent years the measurement of clothing inflation has become one of the more important issues affecting the reliability of the index.

Collecting price data for clothing presents the following challenges:

- Clothing is an aspect of retailing which is highly seasonal. It is common for clothing stores to change large amounts of their stock and product range on a cycle over a season. At its most simplistic we do not expect a clothing store to sell heavy winter coats in the summer months and light summer clothes in the winter. As a result, it is common for products not to be available all year round which presents difficulties for the constant pricing required by local price collection. As retailers also like to make their offerings in clothing fresh each seasonal period, it is not the case, as with some other seasonal goods such as fruit, that a near identical item will be available in the same season of the next year. Fashion retailers do not usually bring back the same range of winter coats each winter, as they will seek to refresh and change the items they offer.

- From a price collection viewpoint, it is hard to know how to replace clothing items with like-for-like replacements even for seemingly simple items within the same shop. For example, a search for "Black Dress" on the website of a major UK retailer in December 2019 revealed 2208 products ranging in price between £7 and £375 and a similar search for "White Shirt" revealed 637 products ranging in price from £3.60 to £65. While it may be clear to most people that the most expensive and least expensive of these items in these categories are not good substitutes for each other, in the middle range of prices the validity of replacing one white shirt with another is much less clear. The temptation is to use price as a guide for which of the substitutes is most relevant; however, this is expressly against the guidelines provided for selecting replacement items for inclusion in the index. Price is not a good guide for the selection of such items because it takes no account of quality differences.
- Clothing is an aspect of consumption where there is a clear fashion element influencing the choices people make, and this makes it hard to identify representative items or close substitutes as items are discontinued or become unavailable. The difficulty can be illustrated by considering two items which are very similar in terms of their raw elements, construction and sales location but can command very different prices depending on how fashionable they are perceived to be by consumers. It is this "fashionability" which presents a particular challenge, as this element cannot directly be identified and measured in the same way that elements like the mix of fabrics can, but it is often critical in determining the price of an individual item. It is also difficult to expect price collectors to be able to judge this attribute of a clothing item in a consistent manner, as it requires a different type of knowledge to that used in other price collections. At its most extreme this issue of fashionability can be considered to have a strong temporal element, where an item of clothing does not have a constant level of "fashionability" across time. Consider for example one of the white shirts priced above. Something may happen to make the lowest priced shirt more (or less) fashionable to consumers, perhaps

a popular celebrity is seen wearing the shirt, or it is featured being worn by a character in a popular TV show, and this means that the desirability of that shirt changes from what it was before that event. In this case the price of the shirt and its physical composition may remain the same but it is, in effect, a different good in the eyes of the consumer. A price collector could not be expected to identify such a change.

- Clothing is an area where there are significant end of season sales, where retailers use pricing discounts to clear remaining stock. The problem this presents is that items can be thought to enter the clothing market at their highest price with prices falling from this point onwards, until stock is all sold out. This introduces a potential downward trend into the part of the RPI which is attempting to measure the change in the price of clothing items, and how to avoid this is a difficult issue for price statisticians. This trend was identified and considered in the work of Greenlees and McClelland (2010), which looked at a large data set from a retailer of clothing in the US market.

Each of the issues noted above can cause significant difficulties for the inclusion of clothing items within a consumer price index. However, it appears that this was not seen as a critical issue in the compilation of the RPI from its inception, and the National Audit Office report of 1990 only raises concern about issues relating to the seasonal elements of clothing and the imputation of prices when items are not available. Clothing did become a significant issue for those compiling the RPI and CPI in 2010 following a change in the way clothing prices were collected, this is described in Chap. 6.

4.5 The Treatment of Electronic Goods, and Hedonics

Electronic goods are products that tend to be complex and change rapidly, this can present problems for traditional price collection methodologies. A new method called "hedonics" was developed to accommodate the complex and changing nature of this type of good (Wells and Restieaux 2014).

The key idea behind hedonics is that the price of an item can be represented as a function of several known and measurable characteristics. Laptop computers are available with a wide range of specifications; it is straightforward to compile a database of laptop prices and for each laptop also to collect key characteristics such as brand, processor speed, size of memory (RAM), size of storage etc. and be confident that we have obtained the key components of the computer which influence its price. A similar approach is applicable to digital cameras and televisions.

Once this data has been compiled, we can build a statistical model which relates the price to each of the characteristics. The useful thing about such a model is that it allows us to price an item of a consistent specification, so for example if a laptop is taken off the market we can still use the model to estimate the price of a laptop of identical specification given the current pricing behaviour in the market. Hedonic methods are a technical approach and their details are not specified here, but Chap. 7 of the International Labor Organisation's Consumer Price Index Manual provides a good overview (ILO et al. 2004).

The technique of Hedonic adjustment became popular among National Statistics Institutes (NSIs) following the Boskin Commission report in 1996. The Office for National Statistics used the technique when examining the price behaviour of laptops, smartphones, tablets, digital cameras and mobile phones from 2003 onwards, although it did stop for digital cameras and mobile phones later on (Wells and Restieaux 2014).

Hedonic modelling is a potentially powerful approach in price measurement, but it is not used widely. One of the reasons for this is the requirements it places on the statistical institute for additional data. However, this cost could fall as automated collection techniques, such as automatic capture of data from websites (web-scraping), become more widespread and easier to apply. Even if this is the case, however, it is likely that hedonic methods will only be used as an exception, rather than the rule in price collection, in part due to the fact that they are more complex and take more time to apply within the tight monthly schedule for producing inflation figures. Their usefulness is greatest in areas where products change very rapidly, which only applies to a limited part of the basket of goods and services used in price collection.

4.6 Owner Occupiers' Housing Revisited

One of the largest and most pressing expenses faced by people is the cost of housing. In the study of consumer price indices, a property is considered to provide "housing services" such as shelter, which occupiers "consume" every month, and so the cost of this should be included in an index of consumer prices as an important area of expenditure. Despite this there have been problems in the inclusion of the cost of housing services for owner occupiers' housing (OOH), where people own or have a mortgage on a property. Note that the problems discussed here are separate from those of measuring the cost of renting properties, which is covered by a separate element of the housing component of the RPI.

One of the most complex problems relating to OOH is that when people buy a house, either outright or through financing secured via a bank or building society, what they are buying is actually a complex set of services and investment products which are not necessarily consumed in the same way as many other goods included in the RPI. When most people buy a house they are purchasing somewhere to live as well as a capital asset which they expect to retain its value through time, and hopefully to appreciate. The question remains then of how to separate the "housing services" they consume from the capital asset element of owning a house and to measure how much the cost of these housing services has changed over the course of time in the RPI.

The original method for including owner occupiers' housing in the RPI was the rental equivalence approach as described in Chap. 3 (Sect. 3.3.3). This was a well-established method, which used the cost of renting an equivalent home as a proxy for the housing services. In the 1970s, concerns arose that the change in equivalent rents wasn't representative of the increases in the cost of mortgage interest payments. The Trades Union Congress wrote to the Advisory Committee in 1975 expressing concerns and the Advisory Committee tasked the Technical Committee with investigating the issue. It concluded that the currently available rental information didn't support the calculation of an appropriate rental equivalence cost. An alternative method based around mortgage interest payments was devised which followed movements in house prices more closely (Department of Employment 1975).

The mortgage interest payments (MIP) element was and remains a significant component of the RPI. Its weight in the index has been as high as 12.3% in 1991, which reflects the importance of such payments for many people covered by the index (ONS 2019b). MIPs cover more than the cost of housing services however, as they are closely related to the financing of a mortgage on a property. They include investment costs and cannot be thought of as a perfect measure for the cost of housing services.

Including MIPs in the RPI caused problems in more recent years, notably around the financial crisis of 2008, where in the 12 months to April

2009 MIPs decreased in size by 46.9%. A contrasting pattern had been seen much earlier in the 12 months to July 1989 when MIPs increased by 63.6% (ONS 2019c). These periods relate to times during which the Bank of England's base interest rate changed radically, with a large increase in 1989, and a significant decrease in 2008/09 (see Fig. 4.1). One of the problems is that the MIPs include an element which is linked to the financing of a property, but not necessarily to the cost of housing services consumed. This can be seen by comparing the cost of rents on housing properties with the MIPs series, as in Fig. 4.2. It can be seen that between 2006 and 2018 prices for rental housing were a lot more stable than MIPs. Since rents are a more direct measure of the costs of housing in a given month, MIPs are clearly not ideal as a measure of the costs of housing services.

As MIPs are such a large element of the RPI it is clear that as MIPs changed in direct response to changes in the Bank of England base rate of interest, the whole index would, to some extent, show the same movement. This feedback loop, where changing the base rate of interest would have a direct influence on the RPI, meant that the RPI was not well suited as a measure of inflation for use in the inflation targeting regime which was introduced in the UK in 1992 (see King 1997 for further information). As a result, RPIX, a variant which stripped out mortgage interest payments

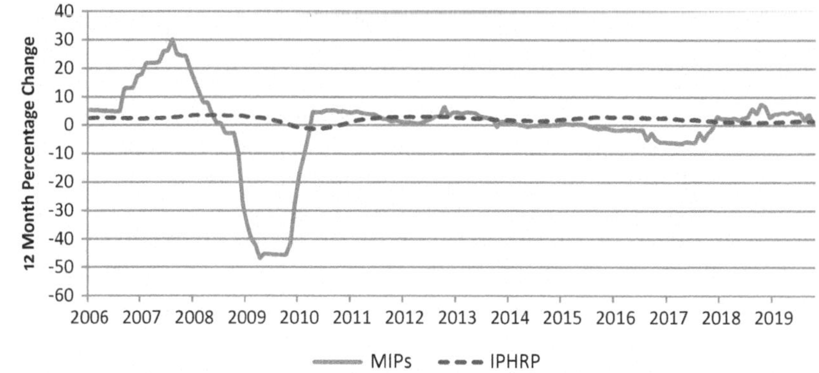

Fig. 4.1 RPI mortgage interest payments, 12 month percentage change 1988–2019. (Source: drawn from: https://www.ons.gov.uk/economy/inflationandpriceindices/timeseries/czcr/mm23)

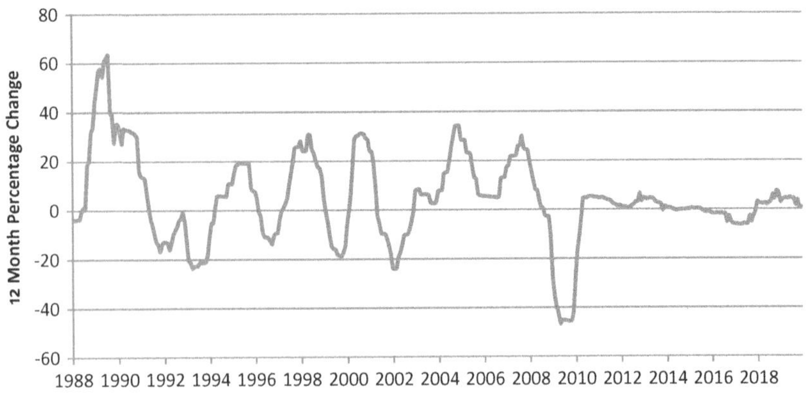

Fig. 4.2 12 month percentage change in MIPs and the Index of Private Housing Rental Prices (IPHRP). (Source: drawn from: https://www.ons.gov.uk/economy/inflationandpriceindices/datasets/indexofprivatehousingrentalpricesreferencetables/current)

from the RPI, was used as the target instead. It would clearly have been inappropriate for the Bank of England to be asked to set Monetary Policy, including the base rate of interest, to manage a level of inflation which they could directly influence as they wished. Indeed, base interest rates are normally increased to reduce inflation, which would cause an increase in the RPI, the opposite of the desired effect.

The situation in which MIPs were used to measure owner occupied housing costs in a measure of inflation was felt by many to be an unsatisfactory method. In recent years there have been renewed discussions of the best approach in the context of the Consumer Prices Index, where the ONS has used a rental equivalence approach to measure the cost of OOH in the CPIH, that is, the CPI including a measure of housing costs (ONS 2018). The approach in the CPIH is to use rental price data to try to approximate how much an owner-occupier would be willing to pay in order to live in the property they inhabit, as was the case initially in the RPI. The seemingly simple question of how to estimate owner occupiers' housing costs has proven historically difficult to answer, particularly in a country like the UK where traditionally there has been relatively sparse information on the rental market for private housing and where a significant part of the population are owner-occupiers.

4.7 Conclusion: Improving the RPI?

In this chapter we have considered the many developments in the methodology of the RPI that took place from the time of its inception. Looking back over all the developments, it is clear that for an index of consumer prices to remain both relevant to the marketplace and to include the best methodology it must have regular expert scrutiny and updating. The RPI has had that level of review by the Advisory Committee and their recommendations were almost always agreed by the government department they reported to and then implemented by the RPI production team.

The treatment of more complex goods such as owner occupiers' housing, clothing and electronic goods also developed over this period. The challenges that these items presented were such that regular detailed reviews were required, and they continued after 1996. The choice of elementary aggregate formula also continued to be a topic of concern and controversy. As the following chapters show, the combination of the formula effect and the measurement of clothing inflation would be a decisive factor in deciding the future direction of consumer price inflation measurement in the UK.

References

Allen, K. (2017, February 17). The UK's inflation foot soldiers: How the ONS measures the CPI. *The Guardian*. Retrieved February 22, 2020, from https://www.theguardian.com/uk-news/2017/feb/12/the-uks-inflation-foot-soldiers-how-the-ons-measures-the-cpi.

Carruthers, A., Sellwood, D. J., & Ward, P. (1980). Recent developments in the Retail Prices Index. *The Statistician, 29*, 1–32.

Central Statistical Office. (1990). *Retail Prices Index Advisory Committee—Treatment of holiday expenditure and other matters in the Retail Prices Index*. Cm. 1156. London: Her Majesty's Stationery Office.

Department of Employment. (1975). *Retail Prices Index Advisory Committee. Housing costs, weighting and other matters affecting the Retail Prices Index*. Cmnd. 5905. London: Her Majesty's Stationery Office.

Department of Employment. (1976). Technical Working Party meeting minutes. LAB 112/20. The National Archives.

Department of Employment. (1977a). Technical proposals for improving the weighting price quotations in the RPI. LAB 112/20. The National Archives.

Department of Employment. (1977b). RPIAC meeting minutes—1977 first meeting. LAB 112/20. The National Archives.

Department of Employment and Productivity. (1968). *A report of the Cost of Living Advisory Committee.* Cmnd. 3677. London: Her Majesty's Stationery Office.

Greenlees, J. & McClelland, R. (2010). *Regression and superlative consumer price indexes for apparel using U.S. scanner data.* Presentation at the 31st General Conference of the International Association for Research in Income and Wealth, St. Gallen, Switzerland, August 27. Retrieved February 25, 2020, from http://www.iariw.org/papers/2010/8amcclelland.pdf.

ILO, IMF, OECD, UNECE, Eurostat & The World Bank. (2004). Consumer price index manual. Geneva: International Labour Office. Retrieved February 25, 2020, from http://www.ilo.org/wcmsp5/groups/public/%2D%2Ddgreports/%2D%2D-stat/documents/presentation/wcms_331153.pdf.

King, M. (1997). The inflation target five years on. Lecture delivered at the London Schools of Economics 29 October 1997. Retrieved February 25, 2020, from https://www.bankofengland.co.uk/-/media/boe/files/speech/1997/the-inflation-target-five-years-on.

National Audit Office. (1990). *The Retail Prices Index.* London: HMSO. Retrieved February 25, 2020, from https://www.nao.org.uk/pubsarchive/wp-content/uploads/sites/14/2018/11/The-Retail-Prices-Index.pdf.

O'Neill, R., Ralph, J., & Smith, P. A. (2017). *Inflation: History and measurement.* Basingstoke: Palgrave Macmillan.

Baxter M. and Camus D. (1998). *Economic Trends*, 543, 25-29. Three year research programme on RPI methodology. Retrieved February 25, 2020, from https://www.escoe.ac.uk/etarticles/et-543-three-year-research-programme-on-rpi-methodology-michael-baxter-dawn-camus-feb-1999/.

ONS. (2012). *Consideration by the ONS of elementary aggregate formulae in the Retail Prices Index: A short history.* Paper released through an FOI request to ONS from what do they know? Retrieved July 30, 2019, from https://www.whatdotheyknow.com/request/correspondence_with_govt_formula#incoming-352140.

ONS. (2018). Consumer Prices Index including owner occupiers' housing costs (CPIH) historical series: 1988 to 2004. Retrieved from https://www.ons.gov.uk/economy/inflationandpriceindices/articles/consumerpricesindexincludingowneroccupiershousingcostshistoricalseries/1988to2004.

ONS. (2019a). RPI: Weights (parts per 1000)—Clothing and footwear. Retrieved from https://www.ons.gov.uk/economy/inflationandpriceindices/timeseries/czhj.

ONS. (2019b). RPI: Weights (parts per 1000)—Mortgage interest payments. Retrieved from https://www.ons.gov.uk/economy/inflationandpriceindices/timeseries/czxe/mm23.

ONS. (2019c). RPI: Percentage change over 12 months—Mortgage interest payments. Retrieved from https://www.ons.gov.uk/economy/inflationandpriceindices/timeseries/czcr/mm23.

Ralph, J., O'Neill, R., & Winton, J. (2015). *A practical introduction to index numbers*. Chichester: Wiley.

Wells, J., & Restieaux, A. (2014). *Review of hedonic quality adjustment in UK consumer price statistics and internationally*. Office for National Statistics. Retrieved February 7, 2020, from https://www.ons.gov.uk/ons/guide-method/user-guidance/prices/cpi-and-rpi/review-of-hedonic-quality-adjustment-in-uk-consumer-price-statistics-and-internationally.pdf.

CHAPTER 5

The RPI in the Political Sphere

Abstract This chapter considers the ways in which the Retail Prices Index (RPI) has been affected by political processes over its lifetime. Political influences were often as important as statistical considerations in determining how and when the RPI developed, both in terms of its status and construction. This chapter places the RPI in context across a range of changes in the political landscape, such as the growing prevalence of inflation targeting as an explicit policy aim of government, the increased harmonisation of measures across the European Union and even the impact of fiscal budget pressures in the US. The results are sometimes surprising; however, it is clear that we cannot ignore the impact of the political sphere on the RPI or vice versa.

Keyword Boskin Commission • Harmonised index of consumer prices • Cost of living framework • Switching inflation measures

Economic statistics are rarely the focus of political life in the modern world, but they are important indicators of the performance of the government of the day. Their role in revealing the impact of policies and in evaluating the state of the nation means that they can be welcomed and highlighted by politicians when they provide news that supports an argument being put forward and downplayed when they don't. This gives a political character to the use of official statistics. In contrast, the

J. Ralph et al., *The Retail Prices Index*,
https://doi.org/10.1007/978-3-030-46563-6_5

methodological choices that statisticians and economists make in the construction of official statistics are not usually controversial nor the subject of public debate. However, aspects of the detailed methodology of inflation statistics did become prominent and hotly debated after 2005. There is a widely held view that the selection and use of inflation measures became a political choice for the next decade or so. The origins of this unusual and uncomfortable situation are found in the events and developments of the 1990s including the state of national finances in the US and greater integration in Europe.

5.1 The Independence of Official Statistics

Overt political influence in official statistics is a rare occurrence. Most countries have high standards of integrity for their official statistics, which are usually produced outside of direct government control. In the UK, the UK Statistics Authority reports to Parliament and not the government, with statisticians required to produce official statistics in an independent and objective manner. There are still residual links to government through the Cabinet Office for the purposes of initiating legislation, and the budget for the Statistics Authority and ONS is set directly by the Treasury, which remains their biggest customer. However, this situation hasn't always been the case. The precursor to the RPI, the Cost of Living Index, was subject to considerable political influence from 1918 to 1945 (Searle 2015); this changed after the Second World War. While the newly created Retail Prices Index was the responsibility of government departments (initially the Ministry of Labour and National Service and later the Department of Employment), its methodology was specified by an expert group—the RPI Advisory Committee, supported by a Technical Committee. These groups met from time to time to consider the methodological issues of the day and their recommendations were put forward to ministers. While the proposals were commented on by ministers and senior civil servants, the final recommendations were almost always accepted. Currently, the RPI is produced by the Office for National Statistics (the executive arm of the UK Statistics Authority) which is a non-ministerial government department. The National Statistician, the chief executive of the ONS, is advised on the procedures for inflation measurement by two expert committees (the Advisory Panels for Consumer Prices, one technical and one stakeholder panel).

The Statistics and Registration Service Act (2007) made the ONS independent of ministers, and set into law that the RPI should be produced monthly. It also set out the procedure for methodological changes to be referred to the Bank of England, who would decide whether they were "a fundamental change in the index which would be materially detrimental to the interests of the holders of relevant index-linked gilt-edged securities", and if so refer it to the Chancellor of the Exchequer for approval. This was a major loosening of the political hold on the RPI, which was specified in the ONS Framework document (HM Government 1996), the document defining ONS role as an agency of government, as:

> In the case of the Retail Prices Index (RPI) special arrangements apply. The scope and definition of the index continue to be matters for the Chancellor of the Exechequer [sic]. The Director will continue to take the lead in advising on methodological questions concerning the RPI and to service the RPI Advisory Committee to which the Chancellor of the Exechequer [sic] will refer issues for consideration as appropriate.

However, the RPI Advisory Committee did not meet after 1997, and developments were discussed between the ONS and Treasury. Although the value of independent official statistics has been recognised for many years, the government has intervened from time to time where concerns have been raised about the quality of official statistics. As described in Chap. 4 (Sect. 4.3), following a mistake in calculating the index, concerns about the accuracy of the RPI led to the National Audit Office undertaking a review in 1990. The resulting report made a number of recommendations to improve the quality of the measure which were acted on (NAO 1990). Apart from this intervention, the period from 1956 to 1996 didn't see the methodology of the RPI high on the political agenda, despite many changes being made. A crucial factor was probably the lack of any competing measure—the Harmonised Index of Consumer Prices (later named Consumer Prices Index in the UK) did not come into being until 1996. There was no direct competitor to the RPI in measuring inflation and so there was little reason for organisations, or individuals, to be concerned about the future of the index.

5.2 The Boskin Commission

In 1995 the Boskin Commission began work in the United States to look into possible measurement errors affecting the US Consumer Prices Index (US-CPI). The Commission's dramatic conclusion was that the measure was overstating the change in the cost of living by 1.1% for the years it considered (Boskin et al. 1996). This substantial bias was made up of contributions from different factors including an insufficient accounting for quality change and the effects of substitution behaviour. While the Commission only considered the US measure, the work carried out by the

Commission was influential in a far wider domain; it highlighted issues caused by the use of certain techniques, particularly the choice of elementary aggregate formula, in the construction of index numbers which influenced price statisticians across the world. The findings of the Commission caused National Statistical Institutes to review their own methodologies and the extent that the factors considered to be contributing to bias in the US might affect their measures.

An important recommendation of the Commission was for the US Bureau of Labor Statistics (BLS) to change its target for measuring the general level of prices to an economic cost of living index; that is, the change in prices to achieve a fixed standard of living rather than the price change of a fixed basket of goods and services. This was a major shift in the target, the BLS accepted the recommendation and gradually moved towards producing a cost of living index. In the UK, the RPI Advisory Committee had considered the target on several occasions in the past. It had been very clear that the target for the RPI was not a cost of living index (Ministry of Labour and National Service 1959; Department of Employment 1986). When the recommendations of the Boskin Commission were examined by the ONS, this rejection of a cost of living index as the target was reiterated. The UK position was that the factors contributing to bias in the US had less effect in the UK; however, research to investigate the issues was instigated (Fenwick 1997).

Chapter 4 (Sect. 4.2) introduced the formula effect, which is a relatively obscure aspect of the methodology concerned with the choice of formula to combine price data at the lowest level of calculation. This is known as the "elementary aggregate level" where there is usually no detailed expenditure weighting information so only prices are combined. This averaging of prices can be carried out with several different formulas (see Appendix A). The Boskin Commission recommended the Jevons, or geometric mean formula, as it was said to better reflect consumer substitution behaviour when relative prices change. The RPI didn't use this formula, it used a combination of two arithmetic formulas—the average of price relatives (the Carli formula) and the ratio of averages of prices (the Dutot formula). In response to the conclusion of the Commission, a number of countries changed their elementary aggregation formulas away from the Carli to the Jevons in their domestic measures of inflation (ONS 2012). Other countries were already using the Dutot formula, which gives very similar results to the Jevons formula; in most cases they didn't change. The UK was one of very few countries that continued to use the Carli formula.

5.3 The Harmonised Index of Consumer Prices

In the 1990s, the European Union (EU) developed a measure of consumer prices which was designed to be comparable across the EU member states. When the elementary aggregation formula for the European measure, the Harmonised Index of Consumer Prices (HICP) came to be specified in 1995, the Jevons and Dutot formulas were recommended. This followed from the fact that most countries had either adopted the Jevons or already had the Dutot index as their elementary aggregate formula for their domestic measures. The Carli was not chosen as it was a formula known to produce results that differed from the Jevons and Dutot formulas when price dispersion is large. The Carli also has unappealing theoretical properties, such as failing the time reversal test (O'Neill et al. 2017, chapter 11). Although the HICP specification did allow other formulas in the index they were required to give results that were close to the Jevons and Dutot, which effectively ruled out the Carli (European Commission 1996). When the UK came to produce its version of the HICP, it was required to use the harmonised methodology which differed from the methodology of the RPI in a number of ways, including the elementary aggregate formula. Calculating a geometric mean of a set of numbers leads to a smaller value than an arithmetic mean (unless all numbers are the same). In almost all cases, therefore, the UK version of the HICP gave a smaller value for inflation than the RPI. The HICP also used a "persons present" coverage, including spending by visitors to the UK and excluding expenditure by UK residents overseas, whereas the RPI covered all spending (including overseas spending) by UK residents only. The UK version of the HICP was named the Consumer Prices Index (CPI) and was first produced in 1997.

Until this point, the RPI had been the only measure of consumer price inflation from its inception in 1956. Once the CPI was published, the situation was different, with two measures produced side by side. While the CPI was originally intended only as the UK version of the HICP, the seed was sown for future disputes about the "best" measure to use. The RPI had been developed and enhanced over decades, but the HICP was effectively created from scratch; it was perceived by many that the HICP used an up to date, internationally approved methodology while the RPI's methodology was "dated". There were aspects of the RPI methodology which could be considered out of step; for example, the use of a classification system for goods and services different to the HICP scheme and the exclusion of low and high-income households. Despite these aspects, viewing the RPI as dated seems a harsh judgement given the extensive efforts that were made to develop and improve its methodology as Chaps. 3 and 4 explain.

The two, essentially political, factors of the Boskin Commission and the introduction of the HICP led to important developments in the UK measures, resulting eventually in the CPI superseding the RPI as the pre-eminent measure of inflation. The Boskin Commission, looking at the state of the US inflation measure was a review driven at least in part by the budgetary needs of the US. A number of key social security programmes saw their levels of payments adjusted in line with inflation and the size of these areas of spending meant that seemingly innocuous changes in inflation could have a significant economic impact. Secondly, the process of harmonising measures of key economic indicators across the European Union required that member states use a common methodology so that the inflation in Germany could be reliably compared to a similar statistic from France and so on. Both the Boskin Commission report and the advent of the HICP saw the Jevons index gain influential status. It is perhaps ironic that subsequent research would suggest that, in the context of consumer price statistics, the use of the Jevons index doesn't model consumer substitution behaviour better than other formulas (Winton et al. 2012). The original belief in the substitution argument followed from consideration of simple economic models of consumer behaviour; this is discussed in Chap. 6. However, the substitution argument wasn't the only one that identified the Jevons formula as a recommended formula to use; the comparability to other formulas and other technical considerations were relevant too (O'Neill et al. 2017, chapter 11).

There is a counter requirement to the need to update the methodology of official statistics and that is to maintain consistency over time. Meaningful comparison between statistics produced at different time periods requires minimal change in the methodology, or advanced analysis. There is a tension between updating statistics to be relevant and leaving them unchanged to ensure comparability, it is likely this is part of the reason why two indices were allowed to persist in the UK.

5.4 An Inevitable Sequence of Events?

The two developments presented above suggest a number of counterfactuals regarding the political situation around the time at which these processes were coalescing. What would have happened had the US not experienced a problematic fiscal deficit in the early 1990s and thus faced pressure to reduce spending? There may not have been a US Commission, and therefore no proposal to adopt the Jevons formula. Secondly what would then have happened if the European Union had not been in the process of seeking a greater level of economic integration? Or if the UK had been more willing to see itself as outside of Europe? In any of these cases the European legislation which required the creation of the HICP may not have had such an impact on inflation measurement in the UK.

It is, of course, entirely possible that without these international drivers, the UK may nevertheless have moved closer to the international consensus in consumer price methodology. Modern statistical practice is a matter of international study and collaboration. As Chap. 4 describes, there were concerns about the use of the Carli formula in the high-inflation era of the 1970s in the UK; the issue was examined in 1975 and the Technical Committee reporting to the RPI Advisory Committee recommended movement away from the Carli to the Dutot for some detailed categories of commodities; this was carried out in 1978. The effects of the Carli formula were studied at regular intervals in the following decades and a further limited change was made in the late 1990s. However, the Carli was never completely removed fom the RPI. There were arguments in favour of the Carli and the problems associated with its use have long been disputed.

The use of the RPI in long term financial instruments such as index-linked bonds and private pensions is a possible reason for the reluctance to make a total switch away from the Carli. It is not implausible that a complete removal of it could have occurred in the 1970s, which would have pre-dated indexed-linked bonds which were first issued in 1981. As Chap. 7 explains, the issue of the Carli formula in the RPI and the difficulty of changing away from the RPI as the indexing measure for long-term financial commitments such as indexed-linked bonds and private pensions never went away and had to be faced eventually.

5.5 Two Measures

The RPI and the CPI had quite different original purposes. The RPI was designed and evolved as a compensation measure; it was used as the basis of wage claims and the adjustment of financial thresholds, compensating for the declining purchasing power of money. In contrast, the CPI (the UK version of the European HICP) was designed as a macroeconomic indicator for use in the process of European integration. Over time, these original uses became blurred. From 1993, a variant of the RPI was used as an inflation target in macroeconomic policy, and gradually the CPI became the preferred measure for compensation purposes.

The situation with consumer price inflation, where there are two alternative measures which are considered to estimate the same quantity, is not a comfortable one. If two measures are applicable to different components of a quantity then there is much less of an issue. For example, having measures of inflation for different social or income groups does not lead to a conflict. The danger of having two measures for one quantity is that a political objective may dictate the choice of which to use rather than a statistical consideration. This risk hasn't been reduced by the ONS, which, as a matter of practice, does not provide guidance on which statistic is best suited for different purposes. Chapter 6 describes the government's gradual adoption of the CPI for indexation purposes, starting with benefits, tax credits and public sector pensions announced in the June 2010 budget.

5.6 The Cost of Living Framework

One of the most confusing aspects of the debate surrounding the use of the RPI is the way in which part of the initial transition between the RPI and CPI was presented. For example, in the process of transitioning Civil Service pension uprating from RPI to CPI it was noted in a number of government produced documents that this was because the CPI better represented the substitution behaviour of consumers than the RPI and so better approximated a cost of living index.

There are several issues to discuss when considering the statement that the CPI better represents a cost of living index than the RPI; there is no single criticism of this argument which we can focus on as several issues are implied by the statement. First of all, it has been made clear that neither the RPI nor the CPI is intended as a cost of living index. This may in part be due to the difficulty which occurs in strictly defining the meaning of the word 'inflation'. To theoretical economists this will quite logically represent a measure which keeps the overall utility level of a reference economic agent constant over time. However these same economists would be hard pressed to argue that this idea can be seen to underpin either the RPI or CPI as they have been formulated. As a result, the idea of criticising either index on this basis is futile, as it can be said that both indices are poor at estimating changes in the cost of living as the term would be interpreted by economists.

The issue regarding the degree to which the substitution behaviour of consumers is better represented by the CPI, because of its use of the

Jevons elementary aggregate formula rather than the Carli, is another area in which it is possible to criticise the statements discussed above. In a very limited case it is possible to show that the Jevons formula is an *exact* measure of the change in the cost of living; however, it is also the case that this *can* be true of the Carli elementary aggregate formula, by using an even more obscure mathematical function to represent the preferences of consumers. The type of theoretical behaviour which is required to produce the Jevons as a cost of living index is extremely limited. This is part of the economic theory that economists meet at the very beginning of their academic career in courses on Microeconomics, though it would be rare for them to consider this material in the specific context of price indices. As a result, it is difficult for anyone to make the argument that the CPI is better able to represent *actual* substitution behaviour based solely on the use of the Jevons rather than the Carli. The source of confidence in this statement might also be traced to the deliberations of the Boskin Commission and to the International Manual for Consumer Prices Indices (ILO et al. 2004) in which the limited practical application of the result is not made abundantly clear to the reader.

Having made the above arguments, we cannot say that the CPI is a better measure of the cost of living, or substitution behaviour, nor can we state the opposite, that the RPI is better in either of these areas. There has not been enough evidence presented to justify either statement; the partial arguments presented above rely on simple models which are unlikely to apply in the complex real world consumer marketplace, as research using detailed consumer panel data showed in 2012 (see Sect. 6.4). The adoption of the CPI as the main measure of inflation in the UK, instead of the RPI, does have justification from other arguments; for example, to maintain consistency with the way in which a key macroeconomic measure was constructed in other countries, and to remove the possible impact of the Carli formula which exhibits undesirable properties in certain circumstances.

5.7 The Adoption of Inflation Targeting

One of the most often quoted, and seemingly most important uses of inflation measures such as the RPI and CPI has been in inflation targeting by the Bank of England Monetary Policy Committee. It is worth noting that such a use could not have been envisaged by the originators of the RPI, as a formal monetary policy regime based on managing the money supply in order to exert control on inflation rates was not a well-known economic policy at the time.

After 1992, the UK switched to a formal monetary policy regime and the RPI (technically the RPIX—a restricted version of the RPI) had a formal role as the target in this process until the decision was made to switch to the CPI as the inflation target in 2003 (HM Treasury 2003). In so doing, it was clear that more emphasis was placed on the recommendation of the Boskin Commission regarding the cost of living than might have been thought important at the time that monetary policy targeting was introduced.

Although potentially one of the most important uses of the RPI, the change in this context does not seem to have met with strong opinions from politicians, economists or the public at large. It is hard to say why this particular decision did not produce much reaction, but it may well have been because the direct impact of such a change was not reflected in people's levels of pay and uprating of their pensions, as we will discuss below. It is also likely that many politicians did not see a need for a grand debate about which index to use as a measure of inflation in this context as it was a largely technical issue and the evidence they were provided with, to support the arguments from HM Treasury, seemed to be clear.

5.8 RPI vs. CPI

One of the interesting things about the differences between the RPI and the CPI, and the fact that their status in the UK has changed over time is that it resulted in the choice of which index to use in a given scenario. This choice became based on expediency, rather than on an attempt to reflect the economic truth of a given scenario. In many cases this meant that opposing parties to a decision chose a different price index, in order to best reflect the case they were arguing. They then could, with some legitimacy, describe this choice as an objective measure by labelling the chosen index as the best measure of inflation.

This has happened at a number of different levels in the economy and the resulting choice of index is often a reflection of which party holds a significant level of power in an economic relationship. As, generally, we can say that the rate of change in the RPI is higher than that in the CPI then, if you are collecting money and want to change payments based on inflation, you would be more likely to favour the RPI as by doing so you would see your stream of payments increase more quickly. Conversely if you are paying money out, it is far more likely that you will want to see your stream of payments increase in line with the CPI, as you will then see your outgoings increase more slowly. Although the difference may "only" be a percentage point or so in a given month this can represent significant amounts of money when we are talking about either large sums of money or changes over a long period of time.

It is helpful to consider an example. In December 2019 the change in the RPI was 0.9% higher than the CPI, a difference which may seem relatively small at first sight.[1] If your pay was increased in line with the December 2019 CPI for 10 years however (at a rate of 1.3%) you would be earning only 91% of what you would have been earning if the RPI for the same period (2.2%) had been used. For many people this would represent a significant loss and so they would much rather use the RPI for uprating their wages in line with 'inflation' than CPI, which is likely to be favoured by their employers.

A disagreement regarding which measure of price change to adopt for changing wages can quickly become a protracted dispute and help to upset industrial relations. For example, at the time of writing, the Universities and College Union were campaigning on a number of issues, including what they see as a cut in real pay, that is pay adjusted for inflation, and they are basing this cut in real pay on the RPI, while University employers offer an amount which they believe is fair given the rate of inflation, as experienced under the CPI.[2] All of this leads to a state of affairs in which the uprating of pay is a political issue between employers and employees and helps to further affect industrial relations in the given sector.[3]

The process of unions and employers using the RPI and CPI respectively in pay negotiations highlights how quickly it is possible for the choice of which statistical measure to use to becomes a political issue. This ability to choose illustrates the damage that not having one definitive measure can do. The context of production and publication are subtle but important factors too. Both measures are produced by the same organisation, the Office for National Statistics, and released on the same day and at the same time. As the CPI gained influence, the ONS changed the order of priority in the statistical output, relegating the RPI to a less prominent place to signal its reduced importance.

[1] See https://www.ons.gov.uk/economy/inflationandpriceindices.

[2] See https://www.ucu.org.uk/he2019-explained.

[3] See https://www.timeshighereducation.com/news/uk-universities-raise-pay-offer-2019-20.

As Chaps. 6 and 7 describe, there was a period where this "inflation measure selection" was clearly evident and it threatened to damage the overall integrity of official statistics. The process by which the RPI was eventually downgraded as an official measure took time and in that period the switch away from the RPI was gradual. During the transition, a few new uses for the RPI were instituted, which only confused the situation further.

There are several areas of life in the UK where use of the RPI has persisted (at the time of writing), for example in the uprating of payments for phone contracts,[4] private rental contracts[5] the uprating of train ticket prices[6] and Student Loan repayments.[7] In contrast, there are other areas where the CPI has been adopted much more quickly, for example when uprating the amount people can earn tax free or when instigating the triple lock for old age pensions. Many of these represent cases where organisations including the government were keener to use the CPI where it pays money out than collects money in. This was discussed during the recent enquiry into the RPI by the House of Lords (UK Parliament 2019) in which representatives of the government made it clear that the use of the effective "margin" represented by the difference in the RPI and CPI was a way to manage the UK's finances or to transfer money from wealthier individuals to less wealthy ones in the case of student loans (see for example the response to Q39 in House of Lords 2018). From a statistical viewpoint, this is clearly unacceptable, but it is understandable that users select the measure they think best suits their needs. It is interesting to note that this practice has been noted in the media but doesn't appear to have caused a great deal of public concern.

5.9 Recent Years

In some ways the existence of the RPI has become more, rather than less, political in recent years. As the methodology of the index began to seem less in step with international thinking on inflation measurement,

[4] See https://www.vodafone.co.uk/explore/costs/rpi/.

[5] See https://www.forbessolicitors.co.uk/news/45135/index-linked-rent-reviews-what-is-it-and-who-benefits.

[6] See https://www.nationalrail.co.uk/times_fares/ticket_types/83871.aspx.

[7] See https://www.gov.uk/repaying-your-student-loan/what-you-pay.

questions were asked about the future of the RPI and whether it should even have one at all.

The long-term uses of the RPI were important factors to be taken into account in trying to resolve the undesirable position where expediency dominated the choice of measure. Those affected by a change in the construction of the RPI, to bring it in line with the CPI, or the replacement of the RPI with the CPI, would emphasise that the use of the RPI is part of a long-term promise to them. As holders of bonds or pensions, they have an expectation of the nature of the indexing and that is the RPI as it is currently calculated. Any scenario where the RPI is changed has a political element, as there will be winners and losers as in most political decisions. The UK government holds about a quarter of its debt in the form of index-linked gilts, which are effectively contracts in which, in some cases, the payments are explicitly linked to the RPI. The regulations around index-linked bonds specify that if the statistical makeup of the RPI is significantly altered then the holders of these gilts must be provided with the opportunity to effectively cash in their contracts with the government early. Faced with this return of debt the government of the day would likely be required to take out more debt on different terms, a process which may be unfavourable to public finances. At the same time, the government would lose the opportunity to use the difference between the CPI and RPI to contribute to a more advantageous fiscal position.

Despite the political difficulties that have held back resolving the issue of having two inflation measures for many years, the weight of opinion has moved to the position where a resolution is needed. This is described in Chap. 7.

5.10 Conclusions

One of the revealing aspects of the story of the RPI and the CPI is that these measures are not "merely statistical entities". They relate to the life of the nation through the economic policies of governments and the decisions of businesses, resulting in effects on individuals; through their uses, inflation measures will always possess a life as political entities. In the recent period of austerity, the indexation of certain benefits was withheld as part of overall government policy. The history, and current status, of the RPI cannot be entirely divorced from the political environment in which it was created, has existed and been used. Understanding the political influences which have shaped the design of the RPI and the uses to which it has been put over its life is important if we are to fully understand the evolution of the statistic over time.

The situation where the choice of inflation measure has not been purely on statistical merits is unusual in the UK, at least in the period of time since the end of the Second World War. The level of political interference in inflation measures has never reached levels which have occurred elsewhere. An extreme example of this comes from Argentina in 2007–2015 in which politicians, and people close to them, attempted to directly interfere with the work of statisticians in producing measures of inflation (Daniel and Lanata Briones 2019), something it would be difficult to imagine if there were not a significant resonance for such an occurrence beyond the statistical world. Although the record of the independence of official statistics in the UK is a good one, it is important for us to realise that measures such as the RPI do not exist in a vacuum and as a result may be subject to a wide range of forces beyond the direct control of statisticians.

References

Boskin, M. J., Dulberger, E. R., Gordon, R. J., Griliches, Z., & Jorgenson, D. (1996). *Toward a more accurate measure of the cost of living.* Retrieved March 1, 2020, from www.ssa.gov/history/reports/boskinrpt.html.

Daniel, C. J. & Lanata Briones, C. T. (2019). Battles over numbers: The case of the Argentine consumer price index (2007–2015). *Economy and Society, 48*, 127–151.

Department of Employment. (1986). *Retail prices index advisory committee. Methodological issues affecting the retail prices index.* Cmnd 9848. London: HMSO.

European Commission. (1996). *Commission regulation (EC) No 1749/96 of 9 September 1996 on initial implementing measures for Council Regulation (EC) No 2494/95 concerning harmonized indices of consumer prices.* Retrieved February 16, 2020, from http://eur-lex.europa.eu/legal-content/EN/TXT/PDF/?uri=CELEX:31996R1749&rid=3.

Fenwick, D. (1997). The Boskin report from a UK perspective. In L. M. Ducharme (Ed.), *Bias in the CPI—Experiences from five OECD countries.* Ottawa: Statistics Canada. Retrieved February 16, 2020 from https://www150.statcan.gc.ca/n1/en/pub/62f0014m/62f0014m1997010-eng.pdf?st=dL4h4M8U.

HM Government. (1996). *Office for National Statistics: Framework Document.* Retrieved May 18, 2020 from https://www.statisticsauthority.gov.uk/wp-content/uploads/2015/12/images-onsframework_tcm97-18283.pdf

HM Treasury. (2003). *Annex: The new inflation target.* Retrieved March 1, 2020, from https://www.bankofengland.co.uk/-/media/boe/files/letter/2003/chancellor-letter-annex-101203.

House of Lords. (2018, July 10). *Select Committee on Economic Affairs uncorrected oral evidence: The use of RPI.* Retrieved March 1, 2020, from http://data.parliament.uk/writtenevidence/committeeevidence.svc/evidencedocument/economic-affairs-committee/the-use-of-rpi/oral/86754.pdf.

ILO, IMF, OECD, UNECE, Eurostat & the World Bank. (2004). *Consumer price index manual.* Geneva: International Labour Office. Retrieved February 25, 2020, from http://www.ilo.org/wcmsp5/groups/public/%2D%2D-dgreports/%2D%2D-stat/documents/presentation/wcms_331153.pdf.

Ministry of Labour and National Service. (1959). *Method of construction and calculation of the index of retail prices* (2nd ed.). London: Her Majesty's Stationery Office.

National Audit Office. (1990). *The Retail Prices Index.* London: HMSO. Retrieved February 16, 2020, from https://www.nao.org.uk/pubsarchive/wp-content/uploads/sites/14/2018/11/The-Retail-Prices-Index.pdf.

O'Neill, R., Ralph, J., & Smith, P. A. (2017). *Inflation: History and measurement.* Basingstoke: Palgrave Macmillan.

ONS. (2012). *International comparison of the formula effect between the CPI and the RPI.* Retrieved February 25, 2020, from https://www.ons.gov.uk/ons/guide-method/user-guidance/prices/cpi-and-rpi/international-comparison-of-the-formula-effect-between-the-cpi-and-rpi.pdf.

Searle, R. (2015). Is there anything real about real wages? *The Economic History Review, 68*, 145–166.

UK Parliament. (2019). *Measuring inflation.* House of Lords Economic Affairs Committee, 5th Report of Session 2017–2019. Retrieved September 15, 2019, from https://publications.parliament.uk/pa/ld201719/ldselect/ldeconaf/246/246.pdf.

Winton, J., O'Neill, R., & Elliott, D. (2012). *Elementary aggregate indices and lower level substitution bias.* Submission for the 2012 IAOS Prize for Young Statisticians. Retrieved February 16, 2020, from http://www.iaos-isi.org/pdf/YSP/2012-2nd-ONeill-Elliott.pdf.

CHAPTER 6

Reviews of the RPI and the Loss of National Statistics Status

Abstract This chapter describes the dramatic events of the period 2008 to 2016 when the difference between the Retail Prices Index (RPI) and the Consumer Prices Index (CPI) came to broad public attention. Two factors drove this. Firstly, a change to clothing price collection instructions unexpectedly widened the RPI—CPI gap and secondly, the government changed the indexing measure for many benefits and pensions from the RPI to the CPI, thereby reducing annual adjustments. This combination resulted in calls for a thorough review of how inflation was measured. An intense period of investigation followed with input from independent experts and several public consultations. This led to the UK Statistics Authority declaring the RPI "a poor measure of inflation". The RPI lost its National Statistics status and its use was strongly discouraged.

Keyword Clothing inflation • Formula effect • Diewert Report • RPI consultation • Johnson Review

6.1 Overview

Previous chapters have shown how the gap between the RPI and the CPI resulted from differences in coverage, the population base and the formulas used at the lowest level of aggregation. Of these differences, it was the formula effect that was responsible for the largest part of the difference. Concerns about the Carli formula were raised in the 1970s and

J. Ralph et al., *The Retail Prices Index*,
https://doi.org/10.1007/978-3-030-46563-6_6

the issue was considered by the RPI Advisory Committee. As a result, the use of the Carli was reduced but not eliminated. It was in the 1990s that the issue of the formula for elementary aggregation was examined again, when it was brought into sharper focus by the introduction of the Harmonised Index of Consumer Prices in 1996, which used the Jevons formula—the geometric mean of price relatives—instead of the Carli. From that time onwards, the formula effect gap was recognised as a concern to statisticians and copious effort went into trying to identify the appropriate formula (or formulas) for use in the RPI and inflation measurement more generally. As described in Sect. 4.2, some changes in the elementary aggregate formula used in the RPI were made in 2003, with 46 elementary indices changed from the Carli to the Dutot (ONS 2012a). However, the gap remained, with a difference between the RPI and CPI in December 2009 of 0.54 percentage points attributable to the use of differing formulas.

While the RPI—CPI gap was being discussed in professional circles before 2010, it hadn't attracted a great deal of public attention. Two quite different events in 2010 changed that in a dramatic way. The first was a revision to the price collection instructions for clothing items, intended to improve the measurement of clothing inflation, but which inadvertently led to a widening of the RPI—CPI gap. Ironically, this didn't arise from a concern about the RPI but from a Eurostat[1] concern about clothing inflation in the CPI. The second event was the announcement by the Chancellor of the Exchequer in his June 2010 budget that the indexation of benefits, tax credits and public service pensions would be switched from the RPI to the CPI from April 2011. Taken together, these changes raised the public profile of the difference between the indices and eventually led to the removal of the RPI's National Statistics status.

6.2 Clothing Inflation

In autumn 2008, ONS was subject to a compliance monitoring assessment from Eurostat. This compliance programme assessed the implementation of the HICP across EU countries; it sought to identify methodological weaknesses and ensure they were addressed (ONS 2009a). The persistent

[1] Eurostat is the statistical office of the European Union, located in Luxembourg.

negative rate of price change for clothing, starting in 1992,[2] exhibited a trend for the UK which differed from the experience of most other EU countries and was raised as a concern to be investigated by ONS. While Eurostat was only interested in the CPI, since the RPI was a domestic measure, any changes to clothing price collection instructions to correct a perceived bias in the CPI were automatically carried through to the RPI as well, since it used the same price data as the CPI.

During 2009, ONS devised changes to the collection instructions for clothing which were intended to improve the quality of the measurement of clothing inflation by removing the source of the perceived underestimation in both the CPI and RPI. The modifications weren't discussed by the recently formed Consumer Prices Advisory Committee,[3] but by the "tripartite group", comprising ONS, the Bank of England and HM Treasury in their December 2010 meeting (ONS 2012a). The changes were:

- Relaxing the rules on acceptable quality changes for replacement items, to achieve an increased sample size
- The collection of sales prices in the January base month to better reflect consumer spending patterns
- Not allowing price collectors to 'mark' an item as temporarily out of stock. Instead a replacement product would be chosen to achieve an increased number of price quotes in the base period

These changes were introduced in January 2010 and resulted in an increased level of clothing inflation in both the RPI and the CPI; however, they also resulted in an increase in the gap between the two indices, as can be seen in Fig. 6.1. In December 2009, the difference was 0.54 percentage points, by December 2010, the difference had grown to 0.86 percentage points, with 0.30 of the additional difference of 0.32 percentage points being attributed to the clothing and footwear division (GSS 2012, pp. 30–48). Figure 6.1 shows the time series of the clothing elements of the RPI and the CPI.

At around the time that the changes to the collection of clothing prices were being introduced, Professor W. Erwin Diewert, an international

[2] Although the CPI was first produced in 1996, a back series was also produced extending back to 1987.

[3] The RPI Advisory Committee wasn't reconvened after 1997 and no replacement committee was formed until 2009, see Sect. 6.2.

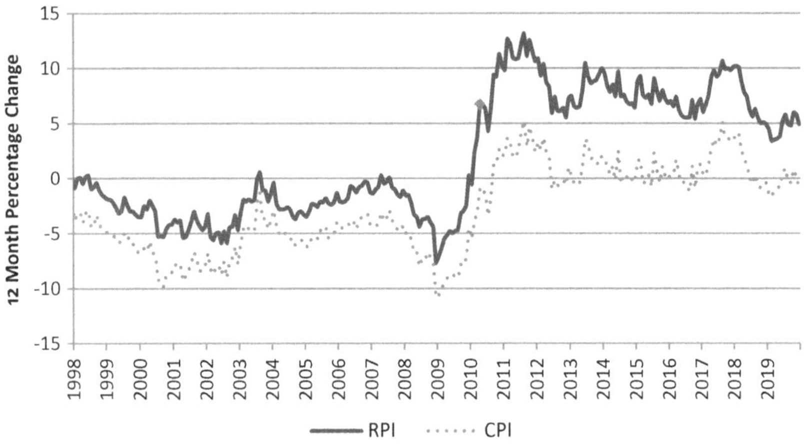

Fig. 6.1 12 month percentage change in the clothing categories of the RPI (CDZ0) and CPI (DKL8) 1989–2019. (Source: drawn from: ONS https://www.ons.gov.uk/economy/inflationandpriceindices#datasets)

expert in Index Numbers, was engaged by ONS to review issues affecting the compilation of inflation measures and in his report (Diewert 2012) he recommended excluding fashion items, such as clothing, with a large fashion element, from the compilation of the index. While seemingly an odd recommendation, it is important to note that Diewert (2012) did not recommend that the entire area of clothing should be removed from the RPI, or the CPI, merely that items which were to a large extent reliant on fashion for their value to consumers should be excluded. Hence if there were items which could be identified as largely unaffected by fashion trends while still being representative of price changes in clothing more generally, they could have been included in the index. Despite this advice and the difficulty of including fashion items in the index, ONS chose to continue with its attempts to include such items, anticipating that its new guidance on price collection would help resolve the issue of the widening of the formula effect.

6.3 Assessing the RPI Methodology

Before the changes to clothing collection instructions were implemented, the various factors behind the differences between the RPI and CPI were discussed at the January 2009 meeting of the tripartite group (ONS

2012a). At this meeting, it was suggested that the methodology of the RPI was out of date and needed to be reviewed. At the time, there was no formal committee making recommendations for the National Statistician on whether to make changes to the methodology of indices of consumer prices. Both the Royal Statistical Society and the tripartite group expressed concern that essential governance for price indices was missing, which would inhibit the ability to make changes to the measures. While the tripartite group was a forum for discussion of price index issues, it was not a formal advisory body. This governance issue was resolved in July 2009 with the formation of the Consumer Prices Advisory Committee (CPAC) whose function was to consider changes and then advise the National Statistician accordingly.

Over the following months, a plan of work was put together by ONS and was discussed at the December meeting of CPAC. The work proposed for 2010 was CPI focused and included work in the areas of owner occupiers' housing for the CPI, temporal coverage of prices and the measurement of seasonal items. Revising the methodology of the RPI was part of the work plan for 2011; topics included a review of the classification framework and population coverage of the RPI with a view to bringing them more into line with the CPI. For elementary aggregates, the work would look at removing the Carli formula, thus eliminating, or at least significantly reducing, the formula effect difference between the two measures (ONS 2009b).

6.4 Public Concerns

A second event, in addition to the change in clothing price collection, brought the formula effect to public notice. This was the decision by the Chancellor of the Exchequer in June 2010 to switch the indexing of many state benefits and pensions from the RPI to the CPI (HM Treasury 2010). This change meant smaller payments than would have been made if the benefits had continued to uprated by the RPI. This raised the issue of the RPI—CPI difference in the consciousness of the general public through newspaper articles which highlighted how much worse off people would be financially as a result of the change.

The significance of the increased formula effect difference and the change of indexing measure were recognised by the Royal Statistical Society (RSS). The RSS president, Professor David Hand, wrote to the chair of the UK Statistics Authority, Sir Michael Scholar, on August 10th' expressing concern that a different "statistical treatment" should result in an effect of such a magnitude (0.86 percentage points) for inflation measures with such widespread uses (Hand 2010). He recommended that ONS investigate the reasons behind the size of the formula effect.

Professor Hand's letter was included in the document pack for the September 2010 meeting of the Consumer Prices Advisory Committee and was discussed at the following meeting in November 2010. Further letters between the RSS and the UK Statistics Authority on the issue followed (UKSA 2010a, b, c; Leyland 2010).

6.5 UK Statistics Authority Assessment Report

Soon after the formation of the UK Statistics Authority in 2007, a monitoring and assessment programme was set up to examine whether official statistics were compliant with the Code of Practice for Official Statistics. Those judged to be compliant with the Code were designated "National Statistics" (UK Statistics Authority 2009, 2018). In April 2010, the assessment team began work on consumer price statistics, reporting their findings in December 2010 (UK Statistics Authority 2010d). This confirmed the National Statistics status of inflation measures, subject to five enhancements, and stated that the measures were produced according to sound methods. However, it noted that it was not always clear that the methods for the RPI, established in the past, were still valid today. It mentioned three areas where changes might be required: the use of entirely arithmetic formulas in the RPI rather than the mix of arithmetic and geometric formulas in the CPI, the classification scheme for items included in the index and the restricted population base of the RPI. The report made five recommendations; the third required work related to the formula effect, directing the ONS to explain the history of the differences between the RPI and CPI, the reasons for these differences and the implications for the uses to which the two measures were put.

The assessment report noted that ONS documentation didn't state whether a particular measure was appropriate for measuring inflation for macroeconomic purposes or for indexation. Indeed, ONS avoided advising on the right measure for specific purposes: "it would not wish to contradict policy adopted by other government departments or private companies in contracts or legal agreements since, by doing so; it could be considered liable for any loss of income resulting from its advice" (UK Statistics Authority 2010e, p. 13). However, it should be recognised that the ONS does not get to define the term inflation in the official sense as this is the prerogative of the Chancellor of the Exchequer.

6.6 ONS Work on the Formula Effect

The appropriate use of the RPI and the CPI was discussed at a public meeting of the Royal Statistical Society held in January 2011. At this session, the ONS presented an overview of the two inflation measures, a summary of the differences between them and their respective uses. The choice of formula at the lowest, elementary aggregate level emerged as a topic of much interest and ONS was encouraged to review the evidence for deciding the most appropriate formula to use.

The UK Statistics Authority Assessment Report, the RSS letter from Professor David Hand and the feedback from the public event at the RSS raised the profile of the need to better understand the differences between the RPI and CPI and in particular, better explain the formula effect and its meaning for the validity of the respective indices. As a result, the ONS began work to better understand and explain the reasons for the formula effect, to explore possible routes to reduce it and to build an evidence base for deciding on the best elementary aggregate formula (or combination of formulas) to use going forward.

An early set of outputs from this work came later in 2011 in the form of three reports covering the uses of inflation measures, the differences between the CPI and the RPI and the history of the differences respectively (ONS 2011a, b, c). A different aspect of the ONS work established a portfolio of research work managed through a project titled: "managing the formula effect". The following sections give a brief overview of the various aspects of this work.

6.6.1 Clothing Inflation Measurement

The increase in the magnitude of the formula effect resulted from changes to instructions for price collection for clothing items. At the May 2011 meeting of CPAC, the ONS presented a paper announcing a further review of the approach to measuring clothing prices. It noted that there were 60 clothing and 12 footwear items included in the indices and while the review would consider overall clothing and footwear price collection, special attention would be paid to those items that contributed most to the formula effect (ONS 2011d). The work would also consider greater stratification by outlet type, replacing strata for independent and multiple location stores with separate strata for prices obtained from supermarkets, high-street stores, discount retailers and department stores. It was thought this might reduce heterogeneity within the strata and so reduce the formula effect, as the difference between the two formulas can be shown to be proportional to the variance of the price relatives used in the construction of the indices.

The ONS created a new set of clothing price collection instructions with tighter specifications for selected items; these were presented to the CPAC meeting in November 2011, along with a proposal from the ONS that a clothing pilot study take place to investigate their effects. This proposal was approved by the committee. The pilot ran alongside the normal collection of clothing prices, which continued to use the collection rules introduced in 2010. The pilot started in February 2012 and the ONS proposed that, should the revised collection instructions reduce the formula effect, they could replace the 2010 instructions as soon as 2013. The relatively tight timescale was a reflection of the concern arising from the increased size of the formula effect and the desire to control what had become an area of controversy. The importance of this work to improve the collection of clothing prices was made clear by a statement from the ONS that the two highest priority items for consumer price index development were the inclusion of owner occupiers' housing in the CPI and improving the measurement of clothing inflation (ONS 2011e, f).

Initial results from the more detailed outlet stratification were presented to CPAC at their February 2012 meeting. Examining price change behaviour for each of the outlet strata revealed differences, suggesting that calculating item indices for these strata separately was appropriate and would reduce dispersion in elementary aggregate measures of price change. However, using the extra outlet stratification made little difference to the formula effect difference between the RPI and CPI methods overall (ONS 2012b).

The initial results of the clothing pilot up to May 2012 were presented to CPAC at its July 2012 meeting. With just a couple of months of data, the revised guidelines had been shown to be effective, resulting in a 12% reduction in dispersion, that is, the variation of prices or price relatives (ONS 2012c). By the time of the September 2012 CPAC meeting, further data had been collected and analysed and was less conclusive regarding the impact of the pilot, with the formula effect gap sometimes smaller and sometimes larger under the new methods (ONS 2012d).

6.6.2 The Formula Effect in Other Countries

Another aspect of the formula effect work saw the ONS review the extent of the formula effect in the inflation measures of other countries (Evans 2012). All EU countries produced both their version of the HICP and also their own domestic measures; however, only Slovenia and the UK used different elementary aggregate formulas in their HICP and domestic measure. The Slovenian HICP used the Jevons formula and the domestic measure used the Dutot; these indices gave similar results leading to an average difference of only 0.1 percentage points in their measurement of inflation between 1998 and 2011. No other EU country used the Carli formula in its domestic index, meaning that the problem of the formula effect was only affecting the UK in this manner. Outside of the EU, very few countries produced more than one general measure.

The ONS also examined changes that had been made by other countries. All countries that had been using the Carli switched to either the Dutot or the Jevons, mainly the latter, as part of the process of beginning to produce the HICP. The reasons given for changing formula included: to keep in line with the HICP, or to better accommodate substitution behaviour, to avoid the lack of transitivity in the Carli and to reduce the potential for upward bias in measures of inflation (Evans 2012, Annex A).

6.6.3 The Diewert Report

To supplement the work to understand and manage the formula effect, in early 2012 the ONS consulted one of the leading authorities on Index Numbers and price statistics: Professor W. Erwin Diewert of the University of British Columbia. He was commissioned by the ONS to:

- Assess the suitability of the RPI and CPI in meeting the purposes for which measures of inflation are generally used
- Identify any weaknesses in either of these indices and make suggestions as to how these weaknesses might be addressed, both in the short term and in the longer run

Professor Diewert visited the ONS in March 2012 and delivered his report in the summer of that year (Diewert 2012). His conclusions were divided into short and long term recommendations.

We only consider the short-term recommendations here; his other recommendations were more technical and not relevant for the scope of this book.

He made the following short-term recommendations:

- Remove the restriction on households included in the RPI—that is the lowest and highest paid; he considered this to be an historical artefact
- Remove the Carli index and replace it with the Jevons; this recommendation was based on the upward bias of the Carli formula relative to other formulas
- Treat fashion goods as strongly seasonal items

Professor Diewert provided a strong steer away from the Carli formula. The Dutot formula was considered acceptable where the strata were narrowly defined, so the spread of price relatives was considered small. The Carruthers, Sellwood, Ward and Dalen (CSWD) formula was also acceptable as a replacement for the Carli—this is the geometric mean of the Carli and the harmonic mean. See Appendix A for the mathematical representation of this and other formulas. While the CSWD formula would be a satisfactory replacement, the adoption of this slightly obscure formula might have added further to the confusion regarding construction of the index.

Section 6.1 discussed the third of the recommendations Professor Diewert made concerned the removal of fashion goods, that is, clothing with a large fashion element governing consumer behaviour, from the compilation of the index. This was a controversial suggestion and wasn't taken forward.

Methods to improve the treatment of clothing have continued to be explored since Professor Diewert's report, though fashion sensitive items are still included in the indices. The ONS has investigated the potential use of new sources for clothing data such as data scraped from retailers' websites and this research has led to an experimental clothing index which better reflects seasonal movements in prices but displays unrealistic falls in price indices (ONS 2017), thus limiting its use in helping with the practical construction of inflation measures.

Measuring clothing inflation effectively and fashion items more generally, continues to be a challenge for price statisticians, and from initial research it is not clear that the increased levels of data available from web-scraping will necessarily resolve the issue. Fashion items therefore remain a problematic area of the RPI (and the CPI), one which is highly likely to have existed for much of its life, but which was only brought to the fore when procedures changed and the difference between the RPI and CPI increased, making the issue more prominent in the minds of those compiling and using the RPI.

6.6.4 *Methodology Work—Economic and Statistical Approaches*

As Chap. 2 described, many different index number formulas have been put forward since the earliest example, the Dutot index formula, was proposed in 1768. Since different formulas give different results and opinions differed as to which of these results was "best", efforts have been made to assess them in a scientific manner with the aim of identifying one, or a small number of "best" performing formulas. A number of different "approaches" have been put forward to try to achieve this noble goal; the three main approaches are the test, economic and statistical, each of which we will now consider.

6.6.4.1 The Test or Axiomatic Approach

The test approach is considered to have been introduced by Walsh (1901), though the classic work on it was written by Irving Fisher (Fisher 1922). In this approach, proposed formulas are assessed against what are considered to be desirable properties, known either as "tests" or "axioms", expressed as functional equations. For example, one of the tests assesses the property of time reversal; this specifies that the product of evaluating an index formula between time periods "0" and "t" and the same formula between "t" and "0" should be equal to one. Among unweighted formulas, the Carli formula fails this test but the Dutot and Jevons pass it, which is the basis for much of the current disapprobation of the Carli formula.

A practical consequence of an index formula failing the time reversal test comes from the case where prices change and return to their previous level. This is sometimes called "price bounce" and in such a situation, it is considered appropriate that an index formula should indicate that no change in the level of prices has occurred (it should be noted that such a bounce happens only when the comparator price is changed between time periods). There will then be a difference between a directly calculated index and a chained index which uses a formula which fails the transitivity test; this difference is known as "drift". Chain drift is the difference between a chained and direct index resulting from the multiplication of index formulas across a link (Clews et al. 2013). Careful use of chaining can keep this drift relatively small. The extent of drift arising from different elementary aggregate formulas is considered in Sect. 6.6.4.3.

Although the test approach appeared a promising way to discriminate between formulas at first, subsequent studies showed that no formula can satisfy all the tests that have been proposed across the literature, and different commentators have come to different views regarding which tests are essential, and which are not, in order for a formula to produce a valid index (Ralph et al. 2015, pp. 169–174). Despite this, time reversal, along with another property, transitivity, has been judged by many experts to be important, though the basis for such a judgement still remains somewhat unclear to others. The failure of the Carli to satisfy both these tests is one of the reasons that some commentators reject the use of the Carli formula and judge that the RPI is a less valid measure of inflation because of its continued use of this formula.

6.6.4.2 The Economic Approach

In the economic approach, utility theory is used to try to determine the index formula that best represents the change in income required to maintain a constant standard of living. The theory is supported by mathematical economics and was used to associate different elementary aggregate formulas with different consumer behaviour (Ralph et al. 2015, pp. 174–184; O'Neill et al. 2017, pp. 265–286). For example, the Boskin Commission claimed that the use of the Jevons formula better reflected situations where consumers substitute alternative goods in response to relative price changes; for example, if pasta became more expensive relative to rice, consumers might be expected to reduce their consumption of pasta. In contrast, the use of the Carli formula was more appropriate where no substitutions were made and items were consumed in fixed proportions (Boskin et al. 1996). This claim was one of the reasons that some NSIs switched formulas to the Jevons.

Like the test approach, the economic approach appeared to provide a rigorous basis for distinguishing between alternative elementary aggregate formulas. However the applied version of this thinking is based on relatively simple models of consumer behaviour. The ONS decided to explore how well these simple models matched real world consumer behaviour using consumer panel data from a market research company. The benefit of panel data is that households typically stay in the "panel", that is, they provide data on their purchases for long periods. This is good for consumer behaviour studies. The approach was reported to CPAC in the September 2011 meeting (ONS 2011g).

The ONS work provided evidence that the simple models of consumer substitution behaviour in response to relative price change are not valid for choosing between the various index formulas. By making changes to the parameters governing preferences and behaviour in economic models it was possible to make any formula the best at approximating consumer behaviour (Winton et al. 2012). This result was reported at the CPAC meeting in April 2012 and effectively removed the economic approach as a means of distinguishing between formulas, although, as we have seen, such reasoning had been used as justification for changing to measurement using the Jevons formula at several points in the history of inflation measurement.

6.6.4.3 The Statistical Approach

There are two aspects to the statistical approach to choosing between formulas: a consideration of the degree to which a sample of price (and quantity) data combined in an index can approximate a population target index and the shape of the distributions of price relatives. The ONS examined both of these aspects, again using real price and quantity data (Elliott et al. 2012) as part of their work into determining the best formula to use. As with the other approaches, there was little to distinguish between the different formulas and this approach provided no clear basis on which to make a definitive recommendation.

6.6.4.4 Other Considerations

With the economic and statistical approaches not providing clear means of distinguishing between the performance of formulas at the elementary aggregate level, the test approach has been considered by some experts and commentators (but not others) to be sufficient to decide between formulas. In some part, this may be due to the fact that it reaches a more definite conclusion than the other methods.

It is easy to identify small datasets which show that the Carli is out of line with other formulas; however, this applies to specific, carefully selected data, which limits its significance and can obscure the relative importance of the issues at hand. It is the case that prices of goods in certain shops go through cycles of being raised and lowered, which has the potential to create bias when the Carli is used (ONS 2018), however the impact of such behaviour is not clear.

The practical impact of using the Carli with a chained index was a potential topic of research; however, with all the other work in progress, it could not be explored before 2013, which meant it was not possible to include findings in the RPI consultation described in Sect. 6.8. The topic is complicated by the fact that linking of the RPI indices occurs above the elementary aggregate level. This does not mean that drift is absent; a little algebra shows that it is still there, it is just less easy to see how it affects the index. Linking the Jevons directly would show no drift as it is a geometric formula, but as it is aggregated with an arithmetic formula (the Lowe index) before linking, some drift will be present when it is used, as in the CPI. It would be expected that the Carli would show larger drift than the Jevons because of its arithmetic nature—the multiplicative nature of linking generates many spurious cross terms. This was the subject of a preliminary study by ONS (in 2013) which did indeed show a greater drift for the Carli than either the Jevons or the Dutot. Drift was calculated for each class of item using the Carli, Jevons and Dutot formulas and the average (absolute) drift for each formula calculated. This showed an average drift of 0.47 for the Carli, with 0.06 for the Jevons and 0.05 for the Dutot, for 2010. This work used local price data only, with an artificial link (Clews et al. 2013).

6.7 Bringing the Work Together

A summary of the various strands of work on the formula effect was brought together at the September 2012 meeting of CPAC. This included the international comparison review, the clothing pilot outcomes, the impact of more detailed outlet stratification, findings on consumer substitution behaviour, the distributions of price relatives and the report from Professor Diewert. In addition, the ONS consulted the Government Statistical Service's Methodology Advisory Committee, Professor Bert Balk of Erasmus University, The Netherlands—another international expert in Index Number theory and price statistics—and an RSS Technical Group assembled to advise ONS in this area.

Although not all of the research was complete, the overall view from the ONS was that, while the revised clothing collection instructions and greater outlet stratification might contribute to reducing the size of the formula effect, it was not likely to make a substantial difference of the size needed to reduce the effect to a negligible concern. The emerging conclusion was that statistical issues and empirical evidence alone would need to be used to decide on the appropriate elementary aggregate formula to use (ONS 2012d). The overall findings were summarised as:

- There is no 'perfect' elementary aggregate formula, nor is there a single, internationally recognised method of determining the most appropriate formula(s)
- There is no statistical reason to use a different formula at the elementary aggregate level for a given item in the CPI and RPI
- The use of the Carli formula is no longer appropriate because of its weak axiomatic properties and susceptibility to bias arising from 'price bounce'

The committee concluded that there was sufficient evidence to consider changing away from the use of the Carli formula in the RPI and advised the National Statistician, Jill Matheson, accordingly. She then proceeded to seek users' views on the findings through a public consultation (ONS 2012e).

Before the consultation took place, the procedure that would follow was set out by the National Statistician (ONS 2012e). The Advisory Committee would meet after the consultation was complete and would advise the National Statistician, who could decide to put forward recommendations for the UK Statistics Authority to consider. Under the terms of the Statistics & Registration Service Act 2007, if a change was recommended, it would need to be considered by the Bank of England to see whether it would result in material, detrimental consequences for holders of index-linked gilts. If this was the case, the Chancellor of the Exchequer would decide whether a change could go ahead. A change to the RPI, if it was recommended and approved, could then take place in March 2013 at the earliest (ONS 2012e).

6.8 The 2012 Consultation

The consultation was launched with the publication of the consultation document on October 8th 2012; it ran until the end of November, after which responses were considered. As well as considering improvements to the RPI, the consultation also included proposals for improving the measures of private rental prices in both the RPI and CPI (ONS 2012e).

Users were invited to give their views on four options for the improving the RPI:

- Make no change in the methodology employed
- Stop using the Carli formula at the elementary aggregate level for clothing only
- Stop using the Carli formula at the elementary aggregate level for all items in the RPI
- Align the formulae used in the RPI at the elementary aggregate level with those used in the Consumer Prices Index (CPI)

The consultation paper asked three questions:

- Which option do you prefer?
- What are the methodological reasons behind your preference?
- Do the options have implications that you would like to draw to the attention of the National Statistician?

Four public meetings were held during the consultation period: in London, Edinburgh, Cardiff and Belfast. In addition, members of the RSS with a particular interest in the topic were invited to meet with the ONS to discuss their views. At the public meetings, the ONS presented the options and attendees were invited to ask questions and present their views.

By the end of the consultation period, a large number of responses had been received—406 in total; 307 were from private individuals and 99 from institutions. A summary of the responses was published in February 2013 (ONS 2013). The counts of preferences for the four options were: 322, 9, 4 and 7 respectively with the rest not expressing a view. The results showed a substantial majority for not making a change. 64 of the responses were statistical and of those, 44 preferred the first option. Many of the other non-statistical responses focused more on the financial impact the decision would have on individuals or organisations.

The reasons for choosing the "no change" option included: the detrimental effect on pensions and investments, and the effects on contracts which may lead to legal action. A few respondents objected to the use of a geometric formula and gave statistical reasons for this. There were some respondents who maintained the traditional view that the respective formulas were linked to substitution behaviour, though there were many who disputed whether this was valid, using a range of arguments. A different view was expressed by those concerned that a change would mean a loss of a long-run, largely consistent series which they valued.

The relevance of the time reversal property was a contested point, not surprisingly. It was Professor Diewert's view that the Carli failing this test was significant. However, others felt that it wasn't an important test and failing it should not rule out the use of the Carli formula. Some respondents noted that a downward bias results from using the Jevons formula in some circumstances, though the nature and extent of this bias was not specified. As well as ONS staff examining the responses, three external experts were asked to review them as well: Professor Diewert, Peter Levell, an economist from the Institute of Fiscal Studies and Professor Denise Osborn from the University of Manchester.

In considering all of the expert advice, research findings and public views, the National Statistician made the following recommendations:

- The Carli formula used in the construction of the RPI "does not meet international standards and a new index should be created". The new index would be known as the RPIJ, with the Carli formula replaced by the Jevons; this would be a version of the RPI which would meet international standards
- The RPI has "significant value to users in maintaining the continuity of the existing RPI's long time series without major change" and should be continued in its current form. This would enable it to continue to be used for long term indexation and for index-linked gilts to meet user expectations

In making her decision, the National Statistician had to weigh the statistical case for a change in formula and all its implications against meeting user needs (the latter being a requirement of the Code of Practice for Official Statistics) through maintaining a long-run series. Maintaining the elementary aggregation formulas would keep the RPI in line with user expectations for index-linked gilts, which was a potentially important practical concern.

The UK Statistics Authority accepted the recommendations of the National Statistician that the formulas used in the RPI should remain unchanged and that a new index, the RPIJ, should be introduced. The decision was announced by the National Statistician at 7 am on January 10th 2013 and the decision was covered widely in the national media.

The RPIJ was formally introduced in March 2013; ONS produced a paper which explained the methodology behind the new index, in particular, where the Carli had been replaced by the Jevons. A back-series was also produced extending back to 1997 (Bird 2013). The new index first appeared in the Consumer Prices statistical bulletin in March 2013 alongside the existing set of indices. The conclusion that the use of the Carli formula in the RPI meant that it did not meet international standards led to a re-assessment of the index by the UK Statistics Authority; this resulted in the RPI losing its National Statistics status.

6.9 The Johnson Review of Consumer Price Statistics

A number of significant changes in the uses of consumer prices had been made in the years since 2000. The replacement of the RPI with the CPI for indexation of benefits, tax thresholds and pensions was perhaps the most visible aspect in the lives of UK citizens. The re-assessment of the RPI and its subsequent change of status was another high profile event, serving to underline this process. By 2013, the UK Statistics Authority felt that it was time for a review of consumer price indices in the UK. In May 2013, Sir Andrew Dilnot, Chair of the UK Statistics Authority, asked Paul Johnson, the head of the Institute of Fiscal Studies (IFS) to carry out a review with the aim of assessing whether consumer price indices were fit to meet current and future needs (UK Statistics Authority 2013a).

At the same time, the UK Statistics Authority announced a review of the governance arrangements for Consumer Price Statistics to be chaired by the deputy chair of the Authority—Professor Sir Adrian Smith (UK Statistics Authority 2013b). The outcome of this review was published in February 2014 and concluded that governance would be best served by two advisory panels—one for technical considerations and one for stakeholder matters such as the applications of consumer price indices. The panels, Advisory Panel for Consumer Prices—Technical and Advisory Panel for Consumer Prices—Stakeholder first met, in joint session, in January 2015.

6.9.1 *Setting the Scope*

To assist Paul Johnson, a small team of experts was assembled with a broad range of experience of official statistics, economics and financial services: John Astin, Bert Balk, Richard Barwell, Robert Hill and Martin Weale were recruited to this group. Two members of staff from the Office for National Statistics provided dedicated support and a number of other ONS staff contributed to the review, drawn from across areas of the ONS including price statistics, economics and methodology.

The terms of reference for the review directed the scope to focus on specific topics, as the extensive underlying methodology and wide range of uses were recognised as being too broad for a review to cover completely. Five specific areas were identified by the UK Statistics Authority (UK Statistics Authority 2013c):

- Recommend a framework for consumer price statistics that will understand and best meet the needs of users, and be accountable, flexible, transparent and no more burdensome than is clearly justified
- Promote recognised and high-quality statistical standards
- Consider the arguments for using cost of living or cost of goods concepts
- Consider how public and private sectors can best work together, using all possible data to maximise quality and efficiency
- Work within the findings of the Authority's review of the governance arrangements and structures supporting the production of price statistics

To keep the scope manageable, the review would not re-examine topics such as the choice of elementary aggregate formula that had been considered in detail in the recent RPI consultation.

With the support of ONS staff there was scope for some original research to be carried out; however, any such work would take time and would need to fit into the timescale of the review; as a result it was necessarily specific and limited. The results of this work would be published alongside the review report.

The original target for completing the review was summer 2014; however, even with a focused scope, the work took longer than expected and the review wasn't completed until January 2015.

6.9.2 General Conclusions of the Review

The Johnson Review considered whether a main measure of inflation should be identified and what it should be. It concluded that there should be a main measure, and that it should be the CPIH, the CPI including the rental equivalence measure of owner occupiers' housing costs, once issues with the rental data had been resolved. The Review recommended that a payments based measure to assess the effects of price changes on different categories of households should also be provided.

Regarding the RPI, the Review agreed that it was statistically flawed through its use of the Carli formula, which can lead to upwardly biased figures for inflation, compared to other unweighted index formulas. While it couldn't be discontinued due to its use in a number of important applications, such as index-linked gilts, commercial contracts and private pensions, the review recommended that the UK Statistics Authority should comment on inappropriate uses when it identified them. It also recommended that users be consulted on discontinuing RPI sub-indices and on whether the development of the RPI should be suspended, except for essential updates such as the basket of goods and services (UK Statistics Authority 2015a).

6.9.3 After the Review Report

The National Statistician, who by this time was John Pullinger, received Paul Johnson's report and its recommendations and took a few months to consider his views about how consumer price indices should be developed. Before deciding on a future course of development, the National Statistician wanted to capture the views of the wider users of these statistics, so he launched a user consultation in June 2015 (UK Statistics Authority 2015b).

The user consultation came in four sections asking for responses to these topics:

- Whether a main measure should be identified and what that should be
- Whether ONS should attempt to measure the inflation experience of different households and how best to do that
- Uses of RPI sub-indices such as RPIY and the Tax and Price Index and whether they could be continued
- The priorities in the ONS work plan and whether council tax should be included in the CPIH

In November 2015, the ONS published a summary of the responses to the consultation (UK Statistics Authority 2015c). There was majority support for a main measure, with CPIH being the most frequently suggested index; others preferred the RPI or the Household Inflation Indices suggested by the Royal Statistical Society (now called Household Costs Indices). Some argued that there should be different measures of inflation for different purposes. There was also strong support for measuring inflation for household types, with the majority preferring a payments approach such as that suggested for the proposed Household Costs Indices. On RPI sub-types, respondents noted that RPIX and RPIY were used in financial contracts with lesser uses of other sub-indices. Many did not want any of the sub-indices to be curtailed.

The National Statistician said he would consider these responses and the advice of his panels (the Advisory Panels for Consumer Prices, one technical and one stakeholder). On March 9th, the National Statistician wrote to Sir Andrew Dilnot, the chair of the Statistics Authority, with a clear statement of his thinking. He was minded to make CPIH the main measure and produce household type measures using the Household Costs Indices which use a payments approach. From the start of 2017, he was considering producing the minimum RPI-related data, stopping RPIJ and making only routine changes to the RPI.

On November 10th 2016, John Pullinger wrote again to Sir Andrew Dilnot. He largely followed his original thinking from March and wrote that he intended to make CPIH the main inflation measure from March 2017, by which time he expected to have resolved the issues from the previous UK Statistics Authority assessment report. A list of which RPI sub-indices would continue and which would cease was published. The RPIJ would cease, though the magnitude of the formula effect would continue to be published and household inflation indices would be developed.

On the 16th November 2016, ONS published a list of which RPI related indices were to be continued and which would be discontinued. The RPI, RPIX, RPI sub-components, composite price index and average price data would continue to be produced. The RPIJ, RPIY, Tax and Price Index and pensioners' indices would be discontinued. In addition, only routine changes would be made to the RPI. Therefore the place of the RPI in the set of inflation measures produced for the UK was weakened and it was expected that only residual uses of the index would continue to be supported. The extent to which this happened is explored in the next chapter.

References

Bird, D. (2013). *Introducing the new RPIJ measure of consumer price inflation*. Retrieved February 29, 2020, from https://webarchive.nationalarchives.gov.uk/20160112014657/http://www.ons.gov.uk/ons/rel/cpi/introducing-the-new-rpij-measure-of-consumer-price-inflation/index.html.

Boskin, M. J., Dulberger, E. R., Gordon, R. J., Griliches, Z., & Jorgenson, D. (1996). *Toward a more accurate measure of the cost of living*. Retrieved March 1, 2020, from www.ssa.gov/history/reports/boskinrpt.html.

Clews, G., Dobson-McKittrick, A., & Winton, J. (2013). *Comparing class level chain drift for different elementary aggregate formulae using locally collected CPI price data*. Retrieved July 31, 2019, from www.ons.gov.uk/ons/guide-method/user-guidance/prices/cpi-and-rpi/comparing-class-level-chain-drift-for-different-elementary-aggregate-formulae-using-locally-collected-cpi-data.pdf.

Diewert, W. E. (2012). *Consumer price statistics in the UK*. Retrieved July 31, 2019, from www.ons.gov.uk/ons/guide-method/user-guidance/prices/cpi-and-rpi/erwin-diewert-report-on-consumer-price-statistics-in-the-uk.pdf.

Elliott, D., O'Neill, R., Ralph, J., & Sanderson, R. (2012). *Stochastic and sampling approaches to the choice of elementary aggregate formula*. Discussion paper. Retrieved February 29, 2020, from https://pdfs.semanticscholar.org/e5e2/48ec183846a0d63ba036e2956e43f9433c69.pdf.

Evans, B. (2012). *International comparison of the formula effect between the CPI and RPI (CPAC(12)07)*. Retrieved July 31, 2019, from https://webarchive.nationalarchives.gov.uk/20160111032628/ http://www.ons.gov.uk/ons/guide-method/development-programmes/other-development-work/consumer-prices-advisory-committee/cpac-papers/cpac-papers%2D%2D-february-2012-meeting.zip.

Fisher, I. (1922). *The making of index numbers: A study of their varieties, tests and reliability*. Boston: Houghton Mifflin.

GSS. (2012). *Managing the formula effect gap between the CPI and RPI*. Government Statistical Service Methodological Advisory Committee 22nd meeting papers. Retrieved February 29, 2020, from https://webarchive.nationalarchives.gov.uk/20160113083327/ http://www.ons.gov.uk/ons/guide-method/method-quality/advisory-committee/2008-2012/22nd-meeting/gss-mac-22-meeting-papers.pdf.

Hand, D. J. (2010). *Letter from Professor David Hand to Sir Michael Scholar*. Retrieved July 30, 2019, from https://www.statisticsauthority.gov.uk/wp-content/uploads/2015/11/letter-from-sir-michael-scholar-to-professor-david-hand-6-october-2010_tcm97-34278.pdf.

HM Treasury. (2010). *Budget 2010*. London: The Stationery Office. Retrieved July 30, 2019, from https://www.gov.uk/government/publications/budget-june-2010.

Leyland, J. (2010). *Letter from Jill Leyland to Sir Michael Scholar*. Retrieved July 31, 2019, from https://www.statisticsauthority.gov.uk/wp-content/uploads/2015/12/letterjillleylandtosirmichaelscholar22021_tcm97-40373.pdf.

O'Neill, R., Ralph, J., & Smith, P. A. (2017). *Inflation: History and measurement*. London: Palgrave Macmillan.

ONS. (2009a). *Eurostat's report on HICP compliance. CPAC(09)7*. Retrieved February 29, 2020, from https://webarchive.nationalarchives.gov.uk/20150910194556/http://www.ons.gov.uk/ons/guide-method/development-programmes/other-development-work/consumer-prices-advisory-committee/cpac-papers/cpac-papers%2D%2D-september-2009-meeting.zip.

ONS. (2009b). *ONS 2010 CPI and RPI development plans. CPAC(09)12*. Retrieved July 31, 2019, from https://webarchive.nationalarchives.gov.uk/20160115180251/http://www.ons.gov.uk/ons/guide-method/development-programmes/other-development-work/consumer-prices-advisory-committee/cpac-papers/cpac-papers%2D%2D-december-2009-meeting.zip.

ONS. (2011a). *How ONS consumer prices are used*. Retrieved July 31, 2019, from https://webarchive.nationalarchives.gov.uk/20170914222346/http://www.ons.gov.uk/ons/rel/cpi/consumer-price-indices/july-2011/how-ons-consumer-price-statistics-are-used.pdf.

ONS. (2011b). *Implications of the differences between the CPI and RPI*. Retrieved July 31, 2019, from https://webarchive.nationalarchives.gov.uk/20170914222346/http://www.ons.gov.uk/ons/rel/cpi/consumer-price-indices/july-2011/implications-of-the-differenced-between-the-cpi-and-rpi.pdf.

ONS. (2011c). *History of and differences between the CPI and RPI*. Retrieved July 31, 2019, from https://webarchive.nationalarchives.gov.uk/20170914222346/http://www.ons.gov.uk/ons/rel/cpi/consumer-price-indices/history-of-and-differences-between-the-consumer-prices-index-and-retail-prices-index/index.html.

ONS. (2011d). *Measurement of clothing prices. CPAC(11)10*. Retrieved July 31, 2019, from https://webarchive.nationalarchives.gov.uk/20160115180251/http://www.ons.gov.uk/ons/guide-method/development-programmes/other-development-work/prices-development-plan/cpac-papers-may-2011-meeting.zip.

ONS. (2011e). *Consumer prices development agenda for 2012. CPAC(11)28*. Retrieved July 31, 2019, from https://webarchive.nationalarchives.gov.uk/20160115180251/http://www.ons.gov.uk/ons/guide-method/development-programmes/other-development-work/consumer-prices-advisory-committee/cpac-papers/cpac-papers%2D%2D-november-2011-meeting.zip.

ONS. (2011f). *Measuring consumer price inflation for clothing. CPAC(11)31.* Retrieved July 31, 2019, from https://webarchive.nationalarchives.gov.uk/20160115180251/http://www.ons.gov.uk/ons/guide-method/development-programmes/other-development-work/consumer-prices-advisory-committee/cpac-papers/cpac-papers%2D%2D-november-2011-meeting.zip.

ONS. (2011g). *Estimating price elasticities. CPAC(11)23.* Retrieved February 29, 2020, from: https://webarchive.nationalarchives.gov.uk/20160111032628/; http://www.ons.gov.uk/ons/guide-method/development-programmes/other-development-work/consumer-prices-advisory-committee/cpac-papers/cpac-papers%2D%2D-september-2011-meeting.zip.

ONS. (2012a). *Consideration by the ONS of elementary aggregate formulae in the Retail Prices Index: a short history.* Paper released through an FOI request to ONS from what do they know? Retrieved July 30, 2019, from https://www.whatdotheyknow.com/request/correspondence_with_govt_formula#incoming-352140.

ONS. (2012b). *Managing the formula effect—Stratification of outlets. CPAC(12)06.* Retrieved July 31, 2019, from https://webarchive.nationalarchives.gov.uk/20160115180251/http://www.ons.gov.uk/ons/guide-method/development-programmes/other-development-work/consumer-prices-advisory-committee/cpac-papers/cpac-papers%2D%2D-february-2012-meeting.zip.

ONS. (2012c). *Progress update on managing the formula effect. CPAC(12)15.* Retrieved July 31, 2019, from https://webarchive.nationalarchives.gov.uk/20160115180251/http://www.ons.gov.uk/ons/guide-method/development-programmes/other-development-work/consumer-prices-advisory-committee/cpac-papers/cpac-papers%2D%2D-april-2012-meeting.zip.

ONS. (2012d). *The formula effect gap between the RPI and CPI. CPAC(12)24.* Retrieved July 31, 2019, from https://webarchive.nationalarchives.gov.uk/20160115180251/http://www.ons.gov.uk/ons/guide-method/development-programmes/other-development-work/consumer-prices-advisory-committee/cpac-papers/cpac-papers%2D%2D-september-2012-meeting.zip.

ONS. (2012e). *National Statistician's consultation on options for improving the Retail Prices Index.* Newport: Office for National Statistics. Retrieved July 31. 2019, from https://webarchive.nationalarchives.gov.uk/20160108013321/http://www.ons.gov.uk/ons/about-ons/get-involved/consultations-and-user-surveys/archived-consultations/2012/national-statistician-s-consultation-on-options-for-improving-the-retail-prices-index/index.html.

ONS. (2013). *Response to the National Statistician's Consultation on options for improving the Retail Prices Index.* Retrieved July 31, 2019, from https://webarchive.nationalarchives.gov.uk/20160108030655/http://www.ons.gov.uk/ons/rel/mro/news-release/rpirecommendations/rpinewsrelease.html.

ONS. (2017). Research indices using web-scraped price data; August 2017 update. Retrieved February 29, 2020, from https://www.ons.gov.uk/economy/inflationandpriceindices/articles/researchindicesusingwebscrapedpricedata/august2017update.

ONS. (2018). *Shortcomings of the Retail Prices Index as a measure of inflation.* Retrieved July 31, 2019, from https://www.ons.gov.uk/economy/inflationandpriceindices/articles/shortcomingsoftheretailpricesindexasameasureofinflation/2018-03-08.

Ralph, J., O'Neill, R., & Winton, J. (2015). *A practical introduction to index numbers.* Chichester: Wiley.

UK Statistics Authority. (2009). *Code of practice for official statistics, Edition 1.0.* London: UK Statistics Authority. Retrieved May 19, 2020, from https://www.statisticsauthority.gov.uk/publication/code-of-practice/

UK Statistics Authority. (2010a). *Letter from Sir Michael Scholar to Professor David Hand.* Retrieved July 31, 2019, from https://www.statisticsauthority.gov.uk/wp-content/uploads/2015/11/letter-from-sir-michael-scholar-to-professor-david-hand-6-october-2010_tcm97-34278.pdf.

UK Statistics Authority. (2010b). *Letter from Sir Michael Scholar to the President of the Royal Statistical Society.* Retrieved May 21, 2020, from https://www.statisticsauthority.gov.uk/wp-content/uploads/2015/11/letter-from-sir-michael-scholar-to-the-president-of-the-royal-statistical-society-061210_tcm97-35471.pdf

UK Statistics Authority. (2010c). *Letter from Sir Michael Scholar to Jill Leyland.* Retrieved July 31, 2019, from https://www.statisticsauthority.gov.uk/wp-content/uploads/2015/12/letterfromsirmichaelscholatojillleyland1904201_tcm97-40371.pdf.

UK Statistics Authority. (2010d). *Consumer price indices—Assessment report 79.* London: UK Statistics Authority. Retrieved May 21, 2020, from https://www.statisticsauthority.gov.uk/wp-content/uploads/2015/12/images-assessment-report-79-consumer-price-indices_tcm97-35275.pdf

UK Statistics Authority. (2013a). *UK consumer price statistics: A review.* Retrieved July 31, 2019, from https://www.statisticsauthority.gov.uk/reports-and-correspondence/reviews/uk-consumer-price-statistics-a-review/.

UK Statistics Authority. (2013b). *Governance of price statistics.* Retrieved July 31, 2019, from https://www.statisticsauthority.gov.uk/reports-and-correspondence/reviews/governance-of-prices-statistics/.

UK Statistics Authority. (2013c). *Review of range of price statistics—Terms of reference.* Retrieved July 31, 2019, from https://www.statisticsauthority.gov.uk/wp-content/uploads/2015/12/images-jrto_tcm97-42927-1.doc.

UK Statistics Authority. (2015a). *Full report: UK Consumer price statistics: A review.* Retrieved July 31, 2019, from https://www.statisticsauthority.gov.uk/wp-content/uploads/2015/12/images-ukconsumerpricestatisticsarevie_tcm97-44345.pdf.

UK Statistics Authority. (2015b). *Measuring consumer prices: The options for change.* Retrieved June 10, 2017, from https://www.statisticsauthority.gov.uk/wp-content/uploads/2015/12/images-consumerpricesconsultationdocumen_tcm97-44662-2.pdf.

UK Statistics Authority. (2015c). *Summary of responses—Measuring consumer prices: The options for change*. Retrieved June 10, 2017, from https://www.statisticsauthority.gov.uk/wp-content/uploads/2015/12/images-summaryofresponsesconsumerpricesconsultatio_tcm97-45027.pdf.

UK Statistics Authority. (2018). *Code of practice for official statistics, Edition 2.0*. London: UK Statistics Authority. Retrieved July 31, 2019, from https://www.statisticsauthority.gov.uk/code-of-practice/.

Walsh, C. M. (1901). *The measurement of general exchange value*. New York: Macmillan.

Winton, J., O'Neill, R., & Elliott, D. (2012). *Elementary aggregate indices and lower level substitution bias*. Statistical Journal of the IAOS, 2013 Vol. 29(1). Retrieved February 29, 2020, from http://www.iaos-isi.org/pdf/YSP/2012-2nd-ONeill-Elliott.pdf.

CHAPTER 7

The Future of the RPI

Abstract This chapter describes the actions of the government in moving indexation from the Retail Prices Index (RPI) to the Consumer Prices Index (CPI). A significant step was made in 2010 when the indexation measure was changed to the CPI for a wide range of taxes and benefits. The government also reconsidered the use of the RPI for bonds and private pensions but after studying the likely consequences decided not to make any change. The continuing use of the RPI, despite it being labelled a "poor measure of inflation" by the UK Statistics Authority, was criticised by the Royal Statistical Society and the House of Lords Economic Affairs Committee in 2018/2019. This led to the announcement by the Chancellor of the Exchequer that the flaws in the RPI would be fixed, but not before 2025.

Keyword Index-linked bonds • Indexing private pensions • Uses of the RPI • House of Lords inquiry • End of the RPI

7.1 Introduction

Chapter 6 told the story of the years 2010 to 2016, when the RPI went from being the measure of choice for the indexing of wages, pensions, contracts, taxes and benefits to being a discredited index. For a statistic that had been in use since 1956, it was a dramatic decline. While Chap. 6 focussed on discussions of the methodology, the 2012 consultation and

J. Ralph et al., *The Retail Prices Index*,
https://doi.org/10.1007/978-3-030-46563-6_7

the Johnson Review, this chapter looks at the implications of the RPI losing its National Statistics status, for all the uses to which the RPI was being put.

The importance of a measure of the general level of prices combined with the long history of the RPI meant that it was employed widely. For some instances where the RPI was used, change would be relatively easy, at least in principle, though not without financial implications. For others, where its use was part of contractual arrangements, change would be harder and it was recognised that replacing the RPI would take an extended period of time.

Here we examine what happened to the RPI since its National Statistics status was revoked and the UK Statistics Authority advised both the public and private sectors to stop using the index as soon as possible. We also examine the extent to which changes have been made and what remains to be addressed.

7.2 Government Uses of the RPI and the Switch to Using the CPI

Many instances where inflation measures were used were in the control of the government; this included adjustments to direct and indirect taxes (or duties), benefits, public sector and state pensions and index-linked government bonds. Given the official advice to move away from the RPI, one would expect that the government would deliver a consistent but cautious move away from the index. We look at the picture in two parts: firstly, the changes prior to the decision in 2013 to remove the National Statistics status from the RPI and secondly the changes made following this date.

7.2.1 Changes Up to 2013

An early change was made as far back as 2003 (HM Treasury 2003). As Chap. 5 (Sect. 5.7) explained, the measure for use as an inflation target was changed from a value of 2.5% using the RPIX (the RPI without mortgage interest) in 2003 to a value of 2% using the CPI. The target value was changed so as to reflect the average difference in magnitude of the RPI and the CPI at the time. This use was for monetary policy purposes and the argument was made that the European HICP (named the CPI in the

UK in December 2003) was designed to be just such a measure. In contrast, the RPI had been developed as an indexing measure for pay and benefits. There was little public reaction to this change as it was seen as a technical move affecting very few people directly.

The years from 2010 to 2012 saw the start of a significant change in the indexing of a wide range of taxes and benefits. The government also considered making changes to allow private pensions to be switched to using the CPI regardless of the terms of pension agreements and followed this up with a consultation on introducing CPI index-linked gilts. If the government had gone ahead with a legislative override for indexing of private pensions and had started to issue CPI index-linked gilts, the move away from the RPI would have seen progress on a wide front. However, the government decided against both a private pension override and issuing CPI index-linked gilts as the following paragraphs explain.

7.2.1.1 Public Sector Pensions, Benefits and Tax Allowances

After the change of inflation target in 2003, the next changes were announced in an emergency budget statement in 2010 (HM Treasury 2010). From April 2011, state pensions, public sector pensions, housing benefits and tax allowances would be uprated using the CPI rather than the RPI. The announcement of this decision provoked much more reaction than the inflation target change as it left many people worse off financially. Although the government argued that the CPI was a more appropriate measure, many people suspected it was simply an opportunistic act to reduce expenditure by switching to an index which was mostly lower in value than the RPI (Telegraph Newspaper 2010).

For state pensions, a protection was added at the same time as the CPI was introduced. The coalition government introduced a "triple lock", where the state pension would rise by the greater of the CPI, average wages or 2.5% (HM Treasury 2010, p. 4). This has continued to be applied, at least up to the end of 2019.

7.2.1.2 Private Sector Pensions

Following the major shift in the indexing measure announced in the 2010 budget, on July 8th the Minister of State for Pensions announced that: "… the government intends to use the CPI as the basis for the statutory minimum revaluation and indexation of occupational pension schemes, and for relevant payments made by the Pension Protection Fund (PPF) and the Financial Assistance Scheme (FAS)" (Department for Work and Pensions 2010a).

In order to see whether wider use of the CPI was practical and/or desirable in private sector pensions, the government carried out a consultation in December 2010. It was acknowledged that many private sector pension schemes had the RPI written into the pension agreements and would therefore be difficult to change. The government invited comment on whether there should be legislative provision to enable the schemes to adopt the CPI in these cases, sometimes referred to as a legislative override. The government's initial position was that it didn't propose to provide such an instrument, but wanted to gain stakeholder views (Department for Work and Pensions 2010b).

The response to the consultation was published by the Department for Work and Pensions in June 2011. While a few respondents were in favour of change, saying that the override would remove the inconsistency arising from differences in the drafting of pension agreements, the vast majority of stakeholders were against the proposal and the government did not proceed. The government noted that there was no fair way to make such a change (Department for Work and Pensions 2011).

7.2.1.3 Index-Linked Gilts

Another consultation was launched in June 2011; this considered the implications of the announcement that the government would change the indexing measure for the statutory minimum revaluation and indexing of private sector pensions from the RPI to the CPI. There was a concern that this move might affect the valuation of pension liabilities and "may affect the preferred choice and type of hedging instruments that schemes use to manage liabilities" (Debt Management Office 2011a, p. 3).

The consultation, launched by the Debt Management Office, was to invite views on whether the government should look to introduce CPI index-linked gilts. To do so, the government would need to be confident of sufficient demand for the new gilts and that the smooth functioning of the market in index-linked debt could be maintained (Debt Management Office 2011a).

The response to the consultation was published in November 2011 by the Debt Management Office. It was decided that issuing CPI index-linked gilts would not be cost effective and would involve risk, so the government did not proceed to issue a mix of RPI and CPI index-linked gilts; however, the government said that the decision would be kept under review. One of the issues raised by stakeholders was that the future inclusion of a measure of owner occupiers' housing into the CPI to create the CPIH may lead to the new index becoming the government's main measure of inflation. Once this had been established then perhaps in the future CPIH index-linked gilts could be introduced (Debt Management Office 2011b).

7.2.1.4 Direct Taxes and Capital Gains Tax

In the 2011 budget document, the government announced a change to the indexation of direct taxes from the RPI to the CPI. On thresholds for "older people", the document states that these would continue to be "over-indexed" by the RPI for the rest of the parliament. This gives a clear picture that the RPI was considered to be over-estimating the adjustment for inflation (HM Treasury 2011). The budget of 2012 contained the announcement that the indexing of the capital gains exempt allowance would move to the CPI from the RPI from April 2013 (HM Treasury 2012).

These changes show a consistent picture of a gradual change in the choice of indexing measure. However, many uses of the RPI remained, including: index-linked government bonds, vehicle excise duty, amusement machine licence duty, gaming duty revalorisation, fuel benefit charges, aviation tax rates and climate change levy rates (HM Treasury 2012).

7.2.2 Uses from 2013

As well as some measures moving away from the RPI, new uses were coming into operation. Interest on student loans was RPI based, as was the indexation of repayments of loans made under "right to buy" schemes. This demonstrated that in 2013, there was a view in some parts of government that where income was concerned, the RPI was the preferred choice, presumably as it gave a higher measure of inflation than the CPI in most circumstances.

The budget of 2013 contained a paragraph that noted the outcome of the National Statistician's consultation on the RPI and explained that the government would keep the use of the RPI for indexation under review while the CPIH and RPIJ became established. It said that index-linked gilts would continue to use the RPI and the government would continue to issue new gilts linked to this index (HM Treasury 2013). This position was maintained through 2014 and 2015; both budget documents for those years made no references to any changes in indexation measures.

Changes recommenced in 2016; the budget document for that year announced that from April 2020, the indexation of business rates would change from the RPI to the CPI (HM Treasury 2016). The following year, the budget document said this change would be brought forward to April 2018 (HM Treasury 2017).

A more detailed discussion of indexing measures was given in the budget document for 2018 which contained a whole page of comment on indexation and set out the future direction of travel. The document noted that the "extensive use of the RPI across both public and private sectors means that moves away from the RPI are complex and potentially costly". For indirect taxes, it stated that a move away from the RPI would lead to substantial costs for the Exchequer. Any further changes are "likely to take place over an extended period of time" (HM Treasury 2018, p. 12). The CPIH was acknowledged as conceptually the best measure of inflation and the government said that it intended to make it the headline measure when it was sufficiently established. The government committed not to introduce any new uses of the RPI (HM Treasury 2018, p. 12).

A further change was made when from May 1st 2019 holders of National Savings & Investments Savings Certificates who wanted to renew an existing Certificate would see the index-linking calculated using the CPI rather than the RPI. Holders were given the option of cancelling (NS&I 2019).

7.2.3 Private Sector Changes

In the private sector, there was also some movement away from the RPI. UKRN is the network of UK regulators, covering a number of regulatory organisations including the Civil Aviation Authority, the gas and electricity regulator, Ofgem, the water regulator, Ofwat, and others. It announced plans to move from the RPI to the CPI or CPIH when setting price controls (UK Regulators' Network 2018).

While the government had rejected the issue of CPI index-linked bonds a bold move was made by Cambridge University. It sold £300 million of CPI indexed-linked bonds in June 2018 together with £300 million at a fixed rate (University of Cambridge 2018).

7.3 More Deeply Embedded Uses of the RPI

This section examines what has happened with some of the other uses of the RPI; these include uses which contain contractual restraints, such as student loan repayments, regulated rail fares and private pension agreements.

7.3.1 Student Loans and Regulated Rail Fares

Student debt on some loans for University education is indexed at rates based on the annual change in the RPI +3%. This has led to high levels of interest being applied and has attracted much criticism, which was voiced in the inquiry held by the House of Lords into the student loans system (UK Parliament 2018a). The former Universities Minister, Jo Johnson, was questioned about the choice of indexing mechanism and the rate. He said that a little known objective of the student loans system was to act as a redistributive tool; this indexation would ensure those earning higher salaries would pay more over time, as the payment is based on the level of salary above a threshold. The relatively high rate of interest was part of the process by which this redistribution would be implemented (UK Parliament 2018b).

Rail fares attract much public attention and annual increases are widely reported in the press. Most fares are set by train companies; however, about 45% are "regulated" by the Rail Delivery Group and rise in January of each year by the level of the RPI in the previous year. Regulated fares include: season tickets and off-peak returns; unregulated fares include advance tickets. In the 2015 budget document, the government said that this use of the RPI was "a cap" intended to "help households with living costs" (HM Treasury 2015).

7.3.2 Private Sector Pensions

The relatively high cost of defined benefit pension schemes has seen their numbers in the private sector decline over time. Typically, they have been closed to new members who are switched into a defined contribution scheme. In many cases, the pension agreements for defined benefit schemes include uprating by the change in the RPI, which is seen to add to their cost. This makes a change to the indexation mechanism attractive to employers. BT and the Barnardo's charity have taken legal action to try to change the indexing measure in their defined benefit schemes.

BT runs several final salary pension schemes; schemes (or "sections") A and B have the CPI as their indexing mechanism while section C has the RPI. This latter section applies to 83,000 members. In court in 2017, the company argued that the de-designation of the RPI by the UK Statistics Authority made the RPI inappropriate for use in indexation of its pension scheme and so the rules allowed it to change the measure. The court disagreed, saying the de-designation did not render the RPI inappropriate and so didn't permit the change. This was upheld in an appeal court ruling in December 2018. The appeal court judge said that the wording in pension agreements was a crucial factor and means a ruling has to be made on a case by case basis. Permission to appeal to the Supreme Court was turned down (Financial Times 2018a).

For Barnardo's, their defined benefit scheme is closed and in deficit; they also wanted to change the indexing from the RPI to the CPI. In September 2015, the high court ruled they couldn't make the change. In February 2017, the court of appeal also ruled that Barnardo's could not change the indexing measure and in November 2017, the Supreme Court unanimously rejected an appeal (Financial Times 2018b).

While employers running defined benefit schemes, whether still open or closed, see advantages in reducing the costs of these pensions by changing the index used, the affected pensioner groups say that the RPI should not be abolished or continue with only routine updates (Sect. 6.8.3); rather the methods should be updated to restore public confidence in the RPI. They argue that where the RPI has been the indexing measure written into pension agreements, this constitutes a promise that uprating will continue to use the RPI, which should be honoured (UK Parliament 2019).

A legislative override was considered by the Department for Work and Pensions in 2010 through a consultation with a response document issued in 2011 as described in Sect. 7.2.1. The decision was not to legislate to provide such a mechanism. This issue was re-considered in 2018 in a government policy paper on protecting defined benefit pension schemes (Department for Work and Pensions 2018). The paper considered the advantages that a switch to the CPI could bring in making final salary schemes sustainable, which would therefore be to the advantage of members of the schemes even if their pension increases were reduced. As in 2011, the government decided not to introduce a legislative override but said that it would keep the issue under review.

7.3.3 *Index-Linked Bonds*

As described in Sect. 7.2.1, the Debt Management Office consulted on the introduction of CPI indexed gilts in 2011 and decided that the risks at the time outweighed the gains (DMO 2011a, b). A more up to date reflection of the current position was provided at a House of Lords inquiry in 2018/2019. Giving evidence on the potential for CPI index-linked gilts, the Chief Secretary to the Treasury, Liz Truss, and the head of the Debt Management Office, Sir Robert Stheeman, both expressed doubts about the viability of a "fragmented RPI and CPI index-linked market". Other stakeholders doubted there would be such an issue (UK Parliament 2019).

7.4 An Unsatisfactory Situation

The initial momentum to replace the RPI starting in 2010 didn't extend beyond 2012. While the government made a series of changes in those years, by the time of the 2013 budget the government said it would keep the use of the RPI under review while waiting for the CPIH and RPIJ to become established (HM Treasury 2013). The use of the RPI in existing index-linked gilts would continue and the government would continue to issue new index-linked gilts using the RPI. The use of the RPI was increased with two new uses introduced by the government in 2013 (see Sect. 7.2.2). Changes to move away from the RPI re-commenced in 2016 and in 2018 the government clarified its position, promising no new uses of the RPI and a gradual move away over an extended period of time (HM Treasury 2018).

On the use of the RPI in private pensions, the legal cases described in Sect. 7.3.2 show that each pension would require its own legal action and the outcomes would depend on the specific wording of the pension agreement, drawn up at a point in the past without any specific consideration of the future implications for indexation.

There were ongoing issues which affected the debate as well. The change in the arrangements for the measurement of clothing prices had inflated the RPI by 0.32 percentage points which resulted in overpayments for gilt holders and those with private pensions indexed by the RPI—as much as a billion pounds a year. This hadn't been corrected.

The position of the UK Statistics Authority was recognised as being difficult. It had a legal obligation to continue to produce the RPI, the only statistic it is legally required to produce under the terms of the Statistics & Registration Service Act 2007 (UK Government Legislation 2007). The UK Statistics Authority also had an obligation to consult the Chancellor about changes to the methodology under the terms of Section 21 of the Act, part 2:

> .... before making any change to the coverage or the basic calculation of the RPI, the Board [in practice, the UK Statistics Authority] must consult the Bank of England. Where proposed changes to the RPI are deemed material and detrimental to relevant gilt holders by the Bank of England, changes cannot be made without the consent of the Chancellor of the Exchequer.

At the same time, the UK Statistics Authority had declared the RPI a poor measure of inflation. Through the 2012 consultation, users had given a strong message that the RPI needed to be maintained in its current form to meet long-term expectations. The UK Statistics Authority was continuing to produce a discredited measure to meet user needs but not meeting its crucial function of ensuring it produced the best possible statistics.

The expectation of the UK Statistics Authority was that the use of the RPI would decline more quickly than it did. However, for indexed-linked gilts and private pension indexing, it looked like there would be no progress in the short to medium term. Overall, this lack of progress was attracting increasing criticism from a variety of sources. In the media, Chris Giles, the economics editor of the Financial Times, had been following the RPI situation for many years and had consistently pressed for government action to resolve the unsatisfactory current position (Financial Times 2019). The inertia was clear to many other stakeholders including parliamentary committees in both houses, the Royal Statistical Society and the Bank of England.

7.5 Royal Statistical Society Meeting in 2018

The complex position with inflation measures was also a concern for the Royal Statistical Society. It hosted a meeting in June 2018 on the future of the RPI. The meeting provided a useful snapshot of opinion. A wide variety of individuals attended, all with a long term interest in consumer price indices. The main speaker was the National Statistician (John Pullinger) with a number of other speakers giving their views (Royal Statistical Society 2018).

The National Statistician explained the route to the current position, where the RPI was considered not to be a good measure of inflation, and the current development plans for consumer price indices. He explained that the UK Statistics Authority perceived two limitations on its actions. Firstly, it could not provide guidance on which measure was appropriate for which use—this choice was up to users (including government), secondly that changing the RPI to fix its problems was not something the Office for National Statistics could do because of its financial consequences—the Treasury would not accept it.

Several speakers described the current position as "a mess" and others expressed frustration that more wasn't being done to sort out the current issues. While the official position was that the RPI was not a good measure of inflation, a number of speakers disagreed and said that an insufficient case had been made. Several pension experts described the difficult position that trustees were currently in with indexing measures. They noted that the question of the future of the RPI was an important one for employers and trustees; the issue was being followed closely as the long term impacts of a change in the indexing measure would be substantial. They called for an agreed, robust measure of inflation that would be stable over an extended period of time.

Other speakers noted the government's declared "direction of travel away from the RPI" but called for more urgent, concerted action to address the more difficult position with index-linked bonds and pensions. They suggested that the government should bring together stakeholders to map out the future path.

The meeting demonstrated the mood with regard to the state of consumer price indices. In summary: the current position was unacceptable and a much greater effort was needed to resolve the issues as a matter of urgency. Users of price indices need clarity and stability over an extended period of time.

7.6 The House of Lords Inquiry, 2018–2019

The growing pressure to resolve the position with respect to the RPI was recognised by their lordships on the Economic Affairs Committee. The origins of their inquiry lay in an annual evidence session which the House of Lords' Economic Affairs Committee held with the Governor of the Bank of England. The Governor, Dr. Carney, suggested that if the committee could advance the cause of reducing the use of the RPI then it would be "a real service". The Committee had scheduled two public hearings on the RPI in June 2018 but concluded that the magnitude of the issues warranted a full inquiry which started in July 2018 and reported in January 2019 (UK Parliament 2019).

The inquiry involved sessions to gather evidence from a range of invited witnesses, and took written submissions. A wide range of organisations and individuals contributed and together their evidence provided a picture of the wide range of views. At the inquiry, the Chief Secretary to the Treasury, Liz Truss, said that while the CPI was generally accepted within government as the best measure of inflation, it was acknowledged that the RPI was "baked into" contracts and pension agreements which could not be changed easily. Even accepting that a transition would need to take place, we would inevitably have to live with the RPI for some time to come. There were examples where a change had been made from the use of the RPI to the CPI; for example, business rates. There was a desire to clear up what could be considered a legacy issue, but it had to be done carefully, weighing costs and risks—a move would be made when it was considered affordable. She noted that the government had frozen some financial measures such as fuel duty rather than index them with the RPI (UK Parliament 2019).

The Economic Affairs Committee asked the Head of the Debt Management Office, Sir Robert Stheeman, whether detailed study had been made of the costs of a "fragmented" market with both types of indexation. He replied that it hadn't, but his feeling was that it would lead to a poorer price for the CPI index-linked gilts. The position would change when a greater number of pension liabilities were linked to the CPI, which was expected to happen gradually; this CPI index-linked liability was growing but was currently small. A future move to a mixed market was supported at the inquiry by Ben Broadbent, the Deputy Governor of the Bank of England, who indicated that there could be CPI indexed-linked bonds in the future (UK Parliament 2019).

7.7 The Issues with the Current Position

The availability of two measures of inflation had resulted in selective use of indices which had undermined the integrity of official statistics. This "index-shopping", as it has been described, brought official statistics and their use into disrepute and was clearly detrimental to public trust. For instances where government sought to generate income, for example in student loan repayments for redistributive purposes, it chose the RPI because its value was usually higher than the CPI. In some cases, the interest rate applied was the change in the RPI + n% to increase the income even further. Instead, the indexing measure could have been the change in the CPI + n + 1% and given much the same result. This might appear a trivial change; however, it would remove another use of the RPI.

Should there be a single measure of inflation? The Johnson Review suggested that there should and that the CPIH, which is based on sound economic principles, should be that measure. That would avoid selective use of inflation measures. For users, there needs to be clarity over which measure should be used for specific purposes. For pension uprating, clarity and stability over long periods of time are desirable (or possibly essential). While any statistical measures will certainly evolve over time as both the economy changes and better methods are developed, managed change should still be acceptable.

The inquiry report on the RPI from the Economic Affairs Committee of the House of Lords was particularly critical of the UK Statistics Authority for not moving to change the RPI sooner. The report said it wasn't the UK Statistics Authority's role to decide that revising the RPI would not be acceptable because of the financial consequences. Their role was to produce high quality statistics; it is government's role to decide whether to implement a change in the use of those statistics. In retrospect, the UK Statistics Authority could have started to develop an experimental, revised RPI years ago. They could then have asked the Chancellor of the Exchequer for permission to replace the RPI with a revised version. It would then have been an issue for the Chancellor as to whether and when a change would be allowed.

7.8 An End to the RPI

The House of Lords report was influential in pushing the UK Statistics Authority and the government to make a statement on the future of the RPI. After the report was issued in January 2019, the head of the UK Statistics Authority, Sir David Norgrove, wrote to the Governor of the Bank of England in February 2019 and the Chancellor of the Exchequer in March 2019, setting out the UK Statistics Authority's plans for the future of consumer price indices (UK Statistics Authority 2019a, b).

Two options were presented for the RPI. The first option would see the production of the RPI cease. This would require primary legislation and would entail actions for the government and many stakeholders to implement a new approach to indexation. The second option was for the methodology to be changed, by adopting the methods used in the CPIH. The RPI would still exist, but would effectively become the CPIH. Sir David asked the Chancellor for consent to either of these changes.

Perhaps not surprisingly, the Chancellor of the Exchequer declined. Two reasons were given: firstly, the significant financial implications of change and the need for a period of time for stakeholders to adjust, and secondly the pressures of delivering Brexit. The Chancellor did, however, accept that change was needed but proposed a date of 2030. He also proposed a consultation to see whether the date could be brought forward to February 2025, and which would also cover the technical aspects of the alignment of the RPI with the CPIH (HM Treasury 2019). At the time of writing, this consultation has been scheduled for March 2020.

7.9 Conclusions

Looking over the whole period of development of measures of the level of prices from their beginnings around 1700 to the present shows just how much had to be put in place to get to what we could call a modern measure. As Chap. 2 describes, while the benefits of such a measure were recognised as early as the 1830s, it took almost a century before the first UK consumer price index was in place—the Cost of Living Index in 1914. Although a big step forward, it was still a relatively elementary measure and it wasn't until after the Second World War with the introduction of the Interim Index of Retail Prices in 1947 and then the Index of Retail Prices in 1956, that we had a "modern measure" with regular updating of the three principal components—prices, weights and basket.

The Retail Prices Index, as it became known, underwent 40 years of development with a larger basket of goods and services, more price quotes and progressively improved methodology. The component of the index related to owner occupiers' housing costs was recognised as the most complex item to include and utilised two approaches along the way. In retrospect, the introduction of the HICP in 1996 marked the beginning of end for the RPI. The Boskin Commission in the US also prompted many countries to examine the methodologies of their domestic measures. Inevitably, having two measures led to fresh questions about the detailed methodology and suitability of each index.

The deficiencies of the RPI became a contentious issue; the relative merits of the Carli, Dutot and Jevons formulas for unweighted indices have been a particular area of disagreement. The appropriate index to use at the lowest, elementary aggregate level of a consumer price index has been debated for many years. Potential issues arising from the Carli formula in the RPI were first noticed in 1975 and this led the ONS to replace it with the Dutot formula for about 30% of items—though it initially suggested the Carli should be removed completely. Further study in 2003 saw more items shifted to the Dutot. Over the period from 1975, there were several occasions when recommendations were made to remove the Carli formula completely. While this would have had consequences, managing them would have been easier than it is today.

By 2009, the RPI methodology was seen as being outdated and a switch from the RPI to the CPI was being discussed. The changes announced in the budget of 2010 showed the government's view, which was that the CPI was the most appropriate measure going forward. Consultations were held on the possibility of a legislative override for replacing the RPI in private sector pension agreements and whether to issue CPI based index-linked bonds in 2011. In both cases, there were good reasons for not making changes; however, if bold steps had been taken to implement the legislative override and start issuing CPI index-linked bonds, the move away from the RPI would have been given a huge push forward.

With the coming of the RPI consultation in 2012, there was a further chance for the removal of the RPI to be accelerated. However, the strong user reaction against change and the need to maintain the RPI for bonds, pensions and contracts led the National Statistician to leave the RPI unchanged, though with the recommendation that users move away from it as soon as possible. In 2013, the government was still using the RPI for indexation in new situations. The government's pace in changing indexing measures slowed considerably from 2013. This was due to the government wanting to see the results of the Johnson Review and to see the completion of the development of the CPIH with its likely future as the main measure of inflation.

Although the situation was difficult for the UK Statistics Authority, a decision to remove or change the methodology could have been taken sooner. This would have required the Chancellor of the Exchequer to make a decision on whether or not to proceed and it is likely that any change would be set for a future date. A period of notice would be needed and subsequent political events may well have meant the timescale would be no different from what it is now (2025 at the earliest). However, this earlier action would have reduced the risk of losing public trust. The government could also have made the decision to stop using the RPI for new purposes earlier and given the message that the use of the RPI would be phased out more prominence.

By 2018, many influential observers were describing the mixed use of the RPI and the CPI as a mess. Some uses of the RPI had been changed, but many remained. There was no immediate prospect of CPI index-linked bonds being issued and the position of indexing in private pensions was described as a lottery, with the choice of measure being determined by detailed wording choices in clauses drafted long ago. Pension experts were calling for clear plans on the future of indexing with long-term stability in the choice of indexing measure. To resolve this unsatisfactory position would need coordination between the government, the statistical authorities and stakeholders.

In the end, the wider statistical community acted, applying pressure to UK Statistics Authority and the government. The Royal Statistical Society and parliamentary committees were particularly influential. The House of Lords Economic Affairs Committee inquiry into the use of the RPI in 2018–19 pushed the UK Statistics Authority and the government into announcing an end to the RPI, at least in its current form—this is likely to happen by 2030.

The difficulties that the government, statistical authorities and users have encountered with consumer price indices are probably the most difficult challenge in the use of official statistics ever faced. The competing demands for measures using the best methodology, fairness between sectors of the user community, continuing to meet well-established (contractual) needs and financial stability have led to a difficult position that has taken and will continue to take many years to unravel.

References

Debt Management Office. (2011a). *CPI-linked gilts: A consultation document.* Retrieved September 15, 2019, from https://www.dmo.gov.uk/media/1977/cons20110629.pdf.

Debt Management Office. (2011b). *CPI-linked gilts: Response to consultation.* Retrieved September 15, 2019, from https://www.dmo.gov.uk/media/14572/cons20111129.pdf.

Department for Work and Pensions. (2010a). *Statement on moving to CPI as the measure of price inflation*. Retrieved September 15, 2019, from https://www.gov.uk/government/news/statement-on-moving-to-cpi-as-the-measure-of-price-inflation.

Department for Work and Pensions. (2010b). *The impact of using CPI as the measure of price increases on private sector occupational pensions schemes. Consultation on government proposals*. Retrieved September 15, 2019, from https://assets.publishing.service.gov.uk/government/uploads/system/uploads/attachment_data/file/220340/cpi-private-pensions-consultation.pdf.

Department for Work and Pensions. (2011). *Government response to consultation—The impact of using CPI as the measure of price increases on private sector occupational pensions schemes. Consultation on government proposals*. Retrieved September 15, 2019, from https://assets.publishing.service.gov.uk/government/uploads/system/uploads/attachment_data/file/185036/cpi-private-pensions-consultation-response.pdf.

Department for Work and Pensions. (2018). *Protecting defined benefit schemes*. Retrieve September 16, 2019, from https://www.gov.uk/government/publications/protecting-defined-benefit-pension-schemes.

Financial Times. (2018a). *BT loses court case over switch to cheaper pension index*. Retrieved September 15, 2019, from https://www.ft.com/content/9ba6155a-f7b7-11e8-af46-2022a0b02a6c.

Financial Times. (2018b). *Barnado's loses legal battle to shift pensions indexation*. Retrieved September 15, 2019, from https://www.ft.com/content/3c0393d0-e27b-11e8-a6e5-792428919cee.

Financial Times. (2019). *MPs slam 'passive' UK Statistics Authority over RPI inflation measure*. Retrieved March 1, 2020, from https://www.ft.com/content/e09cdabe-a88c-11e9-984c-fac8325aaa04.

HM Treasury. (2003). *Annex: The new inflation target*. Retrieved September 15, 2019, from https://www.bankofengland.co.uk/-/media/boe/files/letter/2003/chancellor-letter-annex-101203.

HM Treasury. (2010). *Budget 2010 full text*. London: The Stationery Office. Retrieved September 15, 2019, from https://assets.publishing.service.gov.uk/government/uploads/system/uploads/attachment_data/file/248096/0061.pdf.

HM Treasury. (2011). *Budget 2011 full text*. London: The Stationery Office. Retrieved September 15, 2019, from https://www.gov.uk/government/uploads/system/uploads/attachment_data/file/247483/0836.pdf.

HM Treasury. (2012). *Budget 2012 full text*. London: The Stationery Office. Retrieved September 15, 2019, from https://assets.publishing.service.gov.uk/government/uploads/system/uploads/attachment_data/file/247119/1853.pdf.

HM Treasury. (2013). *Budget 2013 document*. London: The Stationery Office. Retrieved September 15, 2019, from https://assets.publishing.service.gov.uk/government/uploads/system/uploads/attachment_data/file/221885/budget2013_complete.pdf.

HM Treasury. (2015). *Budget 2015 document*. London: The Stationery Office. Retrieved March 1, 2020, from https://assets.publishing.service.gov.uk/government/uploads/system/uploads/attachment_data/file/416330/47881_Budget_2015_Web_Accessible.pdf.

HM Treasury. (2016). *Budget 2016 document*. London: The Stationery Office. Retrieved September 15, 2019, from https://assets.publishing.service.gov.uk/government/uploads/system/uploads/attachment_data/file/508193/HMT_Budget_2016_Web_Accessible.pdf.

HM Treasury. (2017). *Autumn budget 2017*. London: The Stationery Office. Retrieved September 15, 2019, from https://assets.publishing.service.gov.uk/government/uploads/system/uploads/attachment_data/file/661480/autumn_budget_2017_web.pdf.

HM Treasury. (2018). *Budget 2018*. London: The Stationery Office. Retrieved September 15, 2019, from https://assets.publishing.service.gov.uk/government/uploads/system/uploads/attachment_data/file/752202/Budget_2018_red_web.pdf.

HM Treasury. (2019). *Letter from the chancellor of the exchequer to the chair of the statistics authority*. Retrieved September 15, 2019, from https://assets.publishing.service.gov.uk/government/uploads/system/uploads/attachment_data/file/829168/Letter_Cx_Norgrove__4_sept_2019_.pdf.

National Savings and Investments. (2019). *NS&I index-linked savings certificates have changed*. Retrieved September 15, 2019, from https://www.nsandi.com/index-linked-savings-certificates.

Royal Statistical Society. (2018). *The future of the retail prices index*. Retrieved September 15, 2019, from https://events.rss.org.uk/rss/frontend/reg/thome.csp?pageID=67172&ef_sel_menu=1313&eventID=217.

Telegraph Newspaper. (2010). *Pensioners unite to fight switch from RPI to CPI*. Retrieved September 15, 2019, from https://www.telegraph.co.uk/finance/personalfinance/pensions/8161409/Pensioners-unite-to-fight-switch-from-RPI-to-CPI.html.

UK Government Legislation. (2007). *Statistics and registration service act 2007*. Retrieved March 1, 2020, from http://www.legislation.gov.uk/ukpga/2007/18/contents.

UK Parliament. (2018a). *Student loans inquiry*. House of Lords Treasury Committee. Retrieved September 15, 2019, from https://www.parliament.uk/business/committees/committees-a-z/commons-select/treasury-committee/inquiries1/parliament-2017/student-loans-17-19/.

UK Parliament. (2018b). *Student loans inquiry.* House of Lords Treasury Committee. Seventh report of session 2017–2019. Retrieved September 15, 2019, from https://publications.parliament.uk/pa/cm201719/cmselect/cmtreasy/478/478.pdf.

UK Parliament. (2019). *Measuring inflation.* House of Lords Economic Affairs Committee, 5th Report of Session 2017–2019. Retrieved September 15, 2019, from https://publications.parliament.uk/pa/ld201719/ldselect/ldeconaf/246/246.pdf.

UK Regulators Network. (2018). *Position paper on the use of inflation indices.* Retrieved September 15, 2019, from https://www.ukrn.org.uk/wp-content/uploads/2018/11/UKRN-2018-Inflation-paper.pdf.

UK Statistics Authority. (2019a). *Letter to the Governor of the Bank of England (Section 21).* Retrieved September 15, 2019, from https://www.statisticsauthority.gov.uk/correspondence/letter-to-the-governor-of-the-bank-of-england-section-21/.

UK Statistics Authority. (2019b). *Letter to the Chancellor of the Exchequer (Section 21).* Retrieved September 15, 2019, from https://www.statisticsauthority.gov.uk/correspondence/letter-to-the-chancellor-of-the-exchequer-section-21/.

University of Cambridge. (2018). *University of Cambridge raises £600 million in pioneering bonds issue.* Retrieved September 15, 2019, from https://www.cam.ac.uk/news/university-of-cambridge-raises-ps600-million-in-pioneering-bonds-issue.

Appendix A: How Consumer Price Indices are Calculated

This Appendix gives a very brief description of the basic principles that apply to the calculation of consumer price indices. The methodology of the Retail Prices Index follows these principles but has aspects which are specific to it. For example, it excludes data from the wealthiest households and those whose income comes mainly from the state pension (see Section 3.1.1).

The High-Level Principles of Calculating Consumer Price Indices

A sample of all the goods and services available to consumers is chosen—it is called the basket of goods and services. There are about 700 items in the current basket and together they represent all items available to consumers. The basket is updated each year to ensure it both reflects changes in consumer purchasing habits and allows for new products to be included. To calculate a consumer price index, two types of data are required: the prices of goods (and services) and the proportion of expenditure by households on each type of good and service, also called "expenditure shares", or "weights".

Each month, prices for items in the basket are recorded. In most cases, there isn't a single price for each item—the price of an item in the basket can vary according to the particular brand, where it is bought in the UK and the type of retail outlet it is bought from. Prices for items in the basket

J. Ralph et al., *The Retail Prices Index*,
https://doi.org/10.1007/978-3-030-46563-6

are collected across 150 locations and 20,000 retail outlets to reflect these factors. In contrast, central price collection accommodates about 140 items where national pricing policies apply; prices from the internet and catalogues are also collected. In total, 180,000 price quotes are collected each month. The expenditure shares for goods and services are collected through a combination of a survey and administrative data.

A consumer price index is the average price change between time periods with the price changes weighted by the proportion of household expenditure they represent. The formulas in the next section give a little more information on how the calculations are carried out (more than one type of average can be used). A summary of the technical aspects of the calculation is provided by an ONS Technical Manual (ONS 2019). A general introduction to calculating index numbers and consumer price indices is given by one of our previous books (Ralph et al. 2015).

Price Index Formulas

Selecting the formula to combine price changes and expenditure weights is an important and controversial element of the methodology. It has been the subject of investigation and dispute for over two hundred years. International standards have been specified and most countries now follow these standards when calculating their consumer price indices (ILO et al. 2004).

The formulas are of two types: weighted and unweighted. For specific items, such as "800g white sliced loaf bought in an independent store in a specific region", weights are not available and unweighted formulas are used—this is the case for about two-thirds of items.

Unweighted Formulas

$$P_{\text{Carli}}^{0,t} = \frac{1}{N}\sum_{i=1}^{N}\frac{p_{ti}}{p_{0i}} \quad P_{\text{Dutot}}^{0,t} = \frac{\frac{1}{N}\sum_{i=1}^{N}p_{ti}}{\frac{1}{N}\sum_{i=1}^{N}p_{0i}} \quad P_{\text{Jevons}}^{0,t} = \left(\prod_{i=1}^{N}\frac{p_{ti}}{p_{0i}}\right)^{\frac{1}{N}}$$

The RPI uses the Carli and Dutot indices while the CPI and CPIH use the Jevons index in almost all cases with the Dutot for the remainder. In these formulas, p_{0i} and p_{ti} are the prices of the ith item at time periods 0 and t respectively and N is the number of price quotes. The ratios of prices at the two time periods are known as price relatives.

The Carruthers, Sellwood, Ward and Dalen formula is the geometric mean of the Carli and the harmonic mean (the reciprocal of the sum of reciprocals of price relatives):

$$P_{\text{CSWD}}^{0,t} = \sqrt{P_{\text{Carli}}^{0,t} \times P_{\text{harmonic}}^{0,t}}$$

Weighted Formulas

When weighting information is available, the Lowe formula is used:

$$P_{\text{Lowe}}^{0,t} = \sum_{N}^{i=1} s_i^{0b} \left(\frac{p_{ti}}{p_{0i}} \right), \quad \text{where } s_i^{0b} = \frac{p_{0i} q_{bi}}{\sum_{N}^{j=1} p_{0j} q_{bj}}$$

and p_{0i} and p_{ti} are as before. In addition, q_{bi} is the quantity of item i at time period b. s_i^{0b} is the expenditure share of item i with the prices taken from time period 0 and quantities taken from time period b. The Laspeyres index is obtained as a special case when $b = 0$, and the Paasche index when $b = t$ (Ralph et al. 2015).

References

ILO, IMF, OECD, UNECE, Eurostat, & The World Bank. (2004). Consumer price index manual. Geneva: International Labour Office. Retrieved October 27, 2019, from http://www.ilo.org/wcmsp5/groups/public/%2D%2D-dgreports/%2D%2D-stat/documents/presentation/wcms_331153.pdf.

ONS. (2019). *Consumer prices technical manual 2019*. Retrieved October 27, 2019, from https://www.ons.gov.uk/economy/inflationandpriceindices/methodologies/consumerpricesindicestechnicalmanual2019.

Ralph, J., O'Neill, R., & Winton, J. (2015). *A practical introduction to index numbers*. Chichester: Wiley.

Appendix B: Events and Dates

Event	*Date*
Cost of Living Advisory Committee convened	1946
Interim index of retail prices launched	1947
Household income and expenditure survey carried out	1953/54
Index of Retail Prices launched	1956
Family Expenditure Survey started	1957
Annual updating of expenditure weights starts	1962
New group "meals out" created; it was previously split between other groups	1968
Pensioner indices started	1969
Cost of Living Advisory Committee renamed the Retail Prices Index Advisory Committee	1971
The method for calculating owner occupiers' housing costs changed to include mortgage interest payments	1975
New stratification scheme (region and shop type) introduced	1977
Tax and price index introduced	1979
Inflation linked government bonds first issued	1981
Inclusion of UK and foreign holidays	1983/84
New group structure created—durable household goods, miscellaneous and services put into five new groups	1987
Responsibility for the RPI changed from the Department of Employment to the newly reorganised Central Statistical Office	1989
National Audit Office review of the RPI	1990
Office for National Statistics created	1996
Harmonised index of consumer prices (HICP) first published in the UK	1997
Inflation target changed from the RPI to the CPI	2003
Consumer Prices Advisory Committee convened	2009

J. Ralph et al., *The Retail Prices Index*,
https://doi.org/10.1007/978-3-030-46563-6

Event	*Date*
Indexation of state pensions, public sector workers' pensions and many benefits changed from the RPI to the CPI	2010
National Statistician'sconsultation on improving the RPI launched	2012
UK Statistics Authority assessment finds that methods in the RPI are not consistent with international best practice; the RPI loses its National Statistics status	2013
RPIJ introduced; it replaces the Carli with the Jevons formula and so meets international standards	2013
Johnson Review of consumer prices published	2015
Advisory Panels on Consumer Prices convened	2016
RPIJ discontinued; CPIH regains National Statistics status and becomes the ONS's preferred measure	2017
First experimental Household Costs Indices published	2017
House of Lords Economic Affairs Committee inquiry report published	2019
Chancellor of the Exchequer announces that the RPI in its current form will stop in 2030 at the latest	2019

Index

J. Ralph et al., *The Retail Prices Index*,
https://doi.org/10.1007/978-3-030-46563-6

The manufacturer's authorised representative in the EU is Springer Nature Customer Service Centre GmbH, Europaplatz 3, 69115 Heidelberg, Germany. If you have any concerns regarding our products, please contact ProductSafety@springernature.com

Printed and bound by CPI Group (UK) Ltd, Croydon, CR0 4YY
30/09/2026
02225608-0005